Universal Principles
of Storytelling
for Designers

Quarto.com
© 2025 Quarto Publishing Group USA Inc.
Text © 2025 <author if royalty contract>

First published in 2025 by Rockport Publishers, an imprint of The Quarto Group,
100 Cummings Center, Suite 265-D, Beverly, MA 01915, USA.
T (978) 282-9590 F (978) 283-2742

Rockport Publishers titles are also available at discount for retail, wholesale, promotional, and bulk purchase. For details, contact the Special Sales Manager by email at specialsales@quarto.com or by mail at The Quarto Group, Attn: Special Sales Manager, 100 Cummings Center, Suite 265-D, Beverly, MA 01915, USA.

ISBN: 978-0-7603-9246-1

Digital edition published in 2025

eISBN: 978-0-7603-9247-8

Library of Congress Cataloging-in-Publication Data

Names: Sandler, Lyle H., 1960- author.
Title: Universal principles of storytelling for designers : 100 key
  concepts for bringing good ideas to life / Lyle H. Sandler.
Description: Beverly, MA : Rockport Publishers, 2025. | Includes index. |
  Summary: "Universal Principles of Storytelling for Designers provides
  essential storytelling techniques to elevate design projects, making
  them engaging and memorable"-- Provided by publisher.
Identifiers: LCCN 2024046923 | ISBN 9780760392461 (hardcover) | ISBN
  9780760392478 (ebook)
Subjects: LCSH: Communication in design.
Classification: LCC NK1510 .S27 2025 | DDC 744--dc23/eng/20241214
LC record available at https://lccn.loc.gov/2024046923

Design: George Bokhua
Cover Image: David Dron
Page Layout: George Bokhua
Illustration: David Dron

Printed in China

Universal Principles of Storytelling for Designers

100 Key Concepts for
Bringing Good Ideas to Life

Lyle H.
Sandler

ROCKPORT

Contents

Contents
by Category

Introduction

I was about to fly from Los Angeles to New York. It was a few days before Thanksgiving. Three months earlier, I moved to Hollywood and began a Fellowship at the American Film Institute. My studio apartment, blocks from Hollywood Boulevard, with its murphy bed and circa 1970s furniture, lent to the mystique of my new home. Moving here from New York was as different as different could be. But I was in my happy place, immersed in an industry steeped in once upon a times.

In preparation for my flight, I jammed several film scripts into my backpack, intending to read each one during my five-plus-hour flight. I was headed home to spend a few days in reality, where real drama happened as opposed to the shrink-wrapped drama of Hollywood. There would be no opportunities to say cut when someone misbehaved or action when things got dull.

I arrived at my gate as the flight began to board. I took my window seat, and within a few minutes, a man sat down in the aisle seat next to me. I wore a button-down shirt and jeans; my hair was long and thick. I had no idea that male pattern baldness was only months away from taking its grip on me. He was in a suit, with a large briefcase, tightly cut hair, and a newly formed belly that was evidence of too many hours working at a desk. He was at least ten years my senior.

We did the friendly nod thing, acknowledging each other but making a silent commitment not to engage in meaningless banter during the flight. We were soon aloft. As we leveled off at 35,000 feet, we enjoyed a glass of complimentary wine, and we began to engage in the banter we silently agreed not to moments earlier. My seatmate introduced himself as Charles; he had a British accent and invited me to call him Chas. He pulled a large black book from his briefcase. I pulled two scripts from my backpack. While I attempted to focus on my scripts, I could not take my eyes off Chas's tome, a very large unadorned book with black and white pages, and lots of charts. He told me he was an investment banker and, if successful, this would make his firm tens of millions of dollars and himself a big bonus. How do you know it will make you money, I asked and what story does your book tell?

Chas began to share details. He pointed to a pie chart and said the big slice, in red, represented the profits the investors would realize. I asked if red meant to stop or lose rather than gain or go... He said yes, good point, "I'll change it to green – the color of money." I nodded. He breezed through other exhibits, many of which he admitted had nothing to do with the real value of his offering. So why include them? He'd crossed out several pages. I asked who would benefit from this "deal"? When I pushed him just a bit, he told me that the investment would lead to thousands of jobs in Northern California that was devastated by wildfires. Many people lost their homes, farms, and sources of income. He went on to tell me that several new schools would be built as well as homes, and markets that would further economic growth.

I asked Chas to show me where all that great information was in his book. It did not exist. This was a book of numbers, not a story. We began to rethink his story, focusing on how the community was in trouble, how they would benefit from this investment, and how the bank and investors would profit from the region's growth. We identified several individuals, and government officials who would likely stand at the threshold of this initiative to slow it down or stop it for their own benefit. I was back in my comfort zone, writing a story for human consumption.

I was borrowing from my lifelong passion for storytelling. With Chas, I was developing a story that included real people, real life, and real consequences. In due course Chas understood that his story had to progress beyond the bounds of a spreadsheet, and I had an epiphany at 35,000 feet. Until that moment, my world of storytelling and design was about compelling an audience to respond emotionally to fiction; to empathize with fake people, fake places, and fake situations. But I realized I could use my passion for design and storytelling to make a difference in the real world.

As a multidisciplinary designer, I grew my mission over the past twenty-five years. I sought to distill the essence of storytelling for the broader design community, unlocking its transformative potential as a creative form of expression and influence. My aim? To empower fellow designers to craft compelling narratives and leverage storytelling principles to infuse depth and resonance into their work.

The culmination of this effort is presented here in "Universal Principles of Storytelling for Designers." This compilation consists of one hundred principles that underpin storytelling's emotional and value-driven impact. Drawing inspiration from classical theatre, literature, anthropology, psychology, philosophy, and film, these principles are arranged alphabetically and organized into five categories.

•Literary Devices: These tools serve as conduits for conveying meaning, elucidating a story's intent, and influencing human emotions.

•Structure: Representing a story's blueprint, this element systematically orchestrates the sequence of narrative events.

•Emotions: Functioning as resonant threads, emotions are pivotal in guiding humans toward transformative behaviors.

•Psychology + Philosophy : This category provides insights into how humans receive and respond to stimuli, enriching the narrative with depth and resonance.

•Methods/Tools: Encompassing storytelling's mechanical and aesthetic facets, these elements wield significant influence over the transformation process.

Each principle is presented in a two-page layout, with a written composition on the left panel and an illustrative element or text-based descriptor on the right panel. I include a "see also" on most pages that will direct you to other contextually relevant principles within this book.

I will refer to humans in many different ways across these pages, including consumer, user, or audience. When possible, I'll add context. However, in each instance, I refer to the human who is consuming, creating, or embracing a story or a design.

There is no specific order one needs to follow; choose your own journey, perhaps starting with happily ever after and moving to emotion and empathy.

Consider these one hundred principles as a means to bring about human transformation. I hope they inspire your future designs and stories.

Affect as Information Theory

Emotion provides an important source of information for decision-making.

1/100

In crafting a story, designers will undoubtedly focus on form and function, but that alone might not suffice. Humans make decisions by balancing practical considerations with emotions. As you craft your story, consider emotion as a source of information for decision-making. Humans rely on emotion when we lack the ability or motivation to consider all objective factors. In such scenarios, emotions are pivotal when assessing whether a product, service, experience, or design harmonizes with personal preferences, desires, and values.

For instance, an individual apprehensive about flying may choose to take a bus based on their emotions rather than considering the statistically proven fact that air travel is considerably safer than alternative modes of transportation.

Imagine two patients undergoing the same invasive procedure. Both report identical post-procedure discomfort levels. However, Patient One receives post-procedure care marked by empathy and attention, while Patient Two receives only essential care with minimal empathy and a lackluster bedside manner. Patient One enthusiastically confirms their intent to return to the medical practice, whereas Patient Two explores alternative options.

A Gallup study showed that 70 percent of guests at a luxury hotel made decisions based on emotion, with only 30 percent relying on rational factors. The study focused on the significance of physical attributes, such as lobbies and rooms, versus the emotional impact of feeling welcomed and valued.

Consider the following steps to enhance the emotional impact of your story.

1. Employ vibrant language, vivid imagery, and sensory details to ignite emotion.
2. Minimize technical jargon that might overwhelm your audience's cognitive capacity and detract from the story's emotional center.
3. Recognize the subjectivity of emotions; ensure your message resonates as intended by testing it with multiple audiences.
4. Make your story personal by demonstrating your own emotions and authenticity.

See also:
Emotion | Phenomenology | Show, Don't Tell

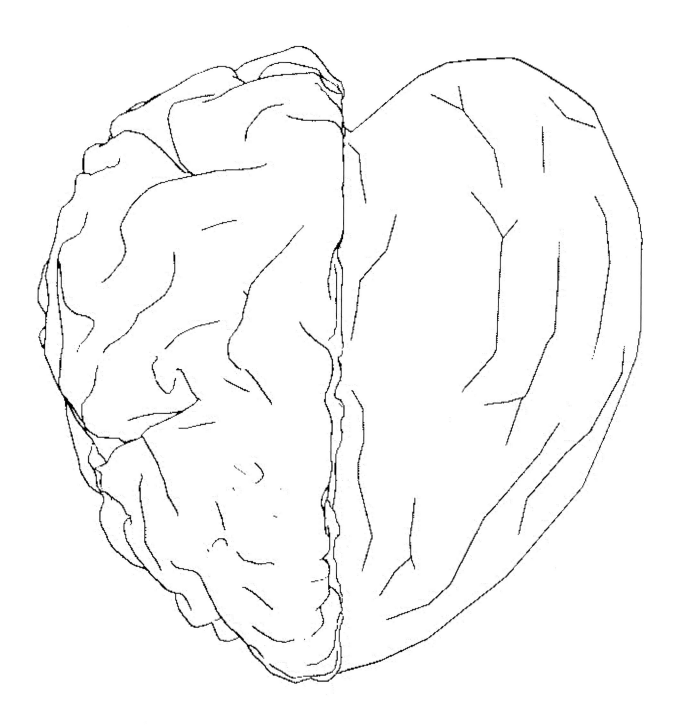

Allegory
A narrative that expresses an alternative or hidden meaning.

2/100

The cover design of the Beatles' *Abbey Road* album is rich in allegory, reminiscent of the longstanding tradition of embedding hidden messages within graphical, literary, and illustrative compositions.

The album cover depicts the four band members casually crossing Abbey Road in London. Delving into the hidden messages, Paul's bare feet sparked a conspiracy theory suggesting his demise in a car accident and replacement with a lookalike on the album cover. Notably, he marches out of step with the rest of the group. The presence of a white Volkswagen with the tag "28IF" adds intrigue, implying Paul would have been twenty-eight years old "if he survived," despite being twenty-seven at the time. A police vehicle, typically linked to traffic fatalities, is parked nearby, and the formation of the four men resembles a funeral procession—with George as the gravedigger, Paul as the deceased, Ringo as the congregation, and John as the priest. This album cover serves as a compelling example of contemporary allegory.

A classic instance of allegorical expression manifests in Pieter Brueghel the Younger's painting, *The Alchemist*. Within this artwork, the alchemist endeavors to transform base metal into gold—an audacious and unattainable pursuit. His wife scours her bag for coins, indicating their desperation for money. A fool can be seen feverishly fanning the flames of the alchemist's fire despite the group's irrational attempt to make gold. In the painting's upper right corner, the alchemist's family begs for coins as if predicting the future, hinting at the dire consequences of the alchemist's imprudent actions leading the family into poverty. Notably, during the 17th century, when this painting was created, alchemy had been discredited. Brueghel's message serves as a warning, cautioning viewers against partaking in such folly, emphasizing that the potential repercussions, involving dishonesty and avarice, are not worth the risk.

Though the concept of crafting allegories may appear antiquated, this technique exposes the inherent value of a concept while encouraging deeper analysis. The success of an allegory lies in the creative transformation of a concrete idea into a semifictional form that heightens its essence and value. While allegories are expected to depict life in an amplified manner, their purpose is not to bewilder or create a narrative that requires strain to decipher. Providing subtle clues within every allegory is imperative, maintaining an element of truth even beneath its seeming abstract surface.

See also:
Analogy (Design by Analogy, DbA) | Metaphors | Archetypes

The success of an allegory lies in the creative transformation of a concrete idea into a semi-fictional form that heightens its essence and value.

Analogy (Design by Analogy, DbA)

The comparison between two things for clarification.

3/100

Design by analogy (DbA) identifies the shared characteristics and purposes between two entities. Many examples of DbA currently exist, the most popular being biomimicry, where the inspiration for a design is inspired by nature. For instance, swimming flippers were inspired by the feet of aquatic birds. The seeds, or burrs, of the burdock plant inspired the hook-and-loop system that enables Velcro to work.

Architecture provides numerous instances of DbA, such as the Wuxi Grand Theatre with its multiple roofs ingeniously inspired by the form of a butterfly. Similarly, the Auditorio de Tenerife Adán Martín replicates the graceful curvature of a palm leaf, while the Yorkshire Diamond Pavilion artfully mirrors the atomic structure of a diamond. Describing the Wuxi Grand Theatre might prove challenging, without acknowledging its inspiration from the butterfly.

Analogies act as a micronarrative, offering instant context for an audience. It is crucial to exercise self-awareness before formulating an analogy, as they have the potential to either elucidate or confound. Additionally, it's essential to consider the influence of language and culture, as they can shape how an analogy is perceived and acted upon. Use analogies to express and simplify the value of a difficult-to-explain concept.

Analogies are about making connections, so include conventional and ordinary phrases that provide strong comparisons.

The following is a list of analogy types.

Part to whole -	Miami is to Florida as New York is to the United States.
Cause to effect -	Snow is to ice as fire is to smoke.
Source to product -	Lemons are to lemonade as water is to ice.
Object to purpose -	Steering wheel is to turn as pen is to write.
General to specific -	Airplane is to 737 as the United Kingdom is to London.
User to tool -	Carpenter is to hammer as artist is to paintbrush.
Synonyms -	Happy is too joyful as angry is to furious.
Antonyms -	Up is to down as left is to right.

See also:
Conflict | Deductions | Metaphors

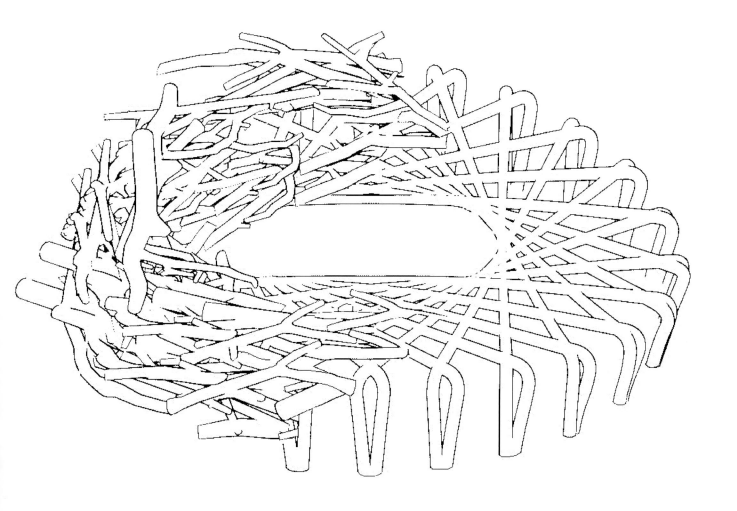

Order and disorder exist in a dynamic relationship.

Anthropomorphism

The application of human characteristics to nonhuman entities.

4/100

During my recent stay at a Chicago hotel, a robot delivered items I requested directly to my room. While I understood these machines lacked life, their anthropomorphic features—a semblance of eyes, a mouth, and a communicative screen—created a compelling illusion of a human interaction. Engaging with these robots felt like a genuine human exchange, complete with the ability to rate its level of service on its screen (suggesting the robot actually cared about the service it was performing).

Much like recognizing faces in clouds or perceiving a friendly smile in a car grill, there's a magnetic allure to designs resembling human features or personalities. Designers often imbue their creations with anthropomorphic qualities. For instance, the 1915 Coca-Cola bottle, known as the "contour" or "Mae West" bottle, was recognized for mimicking the curvature of the female body. This design was not explicit but offered just enough of a clue for customers to identify the human likeness.

Anthropomorphism extends beyond design; it's a potent storytelling tool. Incorporating descriptors that assign human attributes to nonsentient things intensifies the audience's emotional response. This approach aids in memory and awareness and fosters empathy toward nonliving entities. Humans are inherently egocentric and drawn to characteristics reminiscent of themselves, fostering connections with and confidence in nonsentient objects.

I headed up the global design team for an ATM manufacturer. After reviewing hours of security footage, I observed dispassionate ATM users (as dispassionate as the machines they interacted with). Redesigning the entire user experience was impractical, so I focused on evoking emotion without significant changes. We simulated a broken machine. Instead of an undecipherable technical error message on a screen, the malfunctioning ATM displayed the following:

"I am not feeling well. Please visit one of my friends to my left or right."

The response was remarkable. People expressed concern, including one grandmotherly customer who tapped the machine where its head would be and said, "Feel better." This experiment turned a transaction into a relationship and, more importantly, a story. A small, low-cost experiment showcased the power of anthropomorphism in design and storytelling.

See also:
Archetypes | Character Relatability | Personas

Incorporating descriptors that assign human attributes to non-sentient things intensifies the audience's emotional response.

Archetypes

Universal patterns recognizable to all human beings (and Carl Jung).

5/100

"User-centric" is a ubiquitous term in the design world, but "user" lacks the depth of genuine human attributes. Archetypes inject a level of precision and recognizability into the abstract concept of a user, transforming it into a more relatable portrayal. Beyond the individual user, all things designed possess the capacity to be linked with human archetypal traits. Even the most straightforward designs can exhibit traits that mirror the fundamental patterns seen in human archetypes. And some of the most popular brands have adopted archetypal features that infuse vitality into the very essence of the organization they represent.

For example:

Harley-Davidson is recognized as The Rebel.
Jeep has been referred to as The Explorer.
LEGO and Crayola are broadly known as The Creator.

The archetype phenomenon is deeply rooted in our collective unconscious—a theory introduced by Swiss psychiatrist Carl Jung in the early 19th century. The collective unconscious represents instincts common to all humans and, based on our ancestral memories, memories that are inherited or organically passed from generation to generation. What emerged from Jung's theory is a database of human traits that help us better understand with whom and with what we are interacting.

When we encounter individuals, groups, or products demonstrating distinct archetypal traits, a sense of connection, security, and reassurance organically draws our attention. At this point, we decide to approach or avoid.

Design weaves a captivating relationship between its creations and the individuals for whom they are intended, converging within archetypal frameworks. Assigning an archetype to a design will assist in clarifying its personality, value, and approachability. Use archetypal traits in the stories you tell about your designs whenever possible. Take a moment and consider archetypes that could be associated with the humans who surround you; yourself; and the products, services, and experiences you design.

See also:
Character Relatability | Essence Model | Persona

Hero

Caregiver

Creator

Sage

Citizen

Explorer

Innocent

Sovereign

Jester

Lover

Magician

Rebel

Aspiration
The desire or ambition to achieve something.

6/100

Aspirations embody the deep-seated desires of individuals and groups who wish to pursue their goals and dreams. This inner drive prompts contemplation on the steps necessary to overcome challenges that may appear daunting—if not insurmountable—in pursuit of aspirations. Consequently, nothing is more gratifying than encountering something, someone, or a story that enables or hastens the realization of an aspiration. This is where the intersection of design and storytelling becomes pivotal.

Integrating aspirations into design narratives instills hope, making seemingly daunting goals attainable. Successful aspirational narratives fortify the bond with consumers and unveil heightened levels of empathy. Numerous brands showcase their adept understanding of consumer aspirations by skillfully blending design and storytelling, creating a compelling and resonant experience.

For instance, take Patagonia, the esteemed outdoor clothing and gear company. It forges a profound connection with its clientele by skillfully crafting aspirational narratives, like "Say Goodbye to Forever Chemicals" and "All the Hemp That Fits." These narratives serve as a vibrant showcase, shedding light on the environmental benefits of cultivating hemp and the health advantages of a chemical-free product line. Patagonia's design ethos aligns seamlessly with the aspirations of its consumers to embrace environmental friendliness, and it tells that story very well.

This commitment extends beyond the digital realm, finding tangible expression in physical stores that tran-

scend traditional storytelling. Patagonia's dedication to the environment permeates its retail spaces, characterized by natural finishes, wide-open spaces, and tangible evidence of its environmental pledge. Patagonia goes beyond the transaction of goods and services, extending a commitment to its consumers to help them achieve their environmental aspirations.

When constructing an aspirational narrative, unveiling its purpose before its utility is crucial. Purpose describes the intent of the aspiration, not its technical attributes. To seamlessly integrate aspirations into your narrative, ponder these questions:

1. Who are the individuals you seek to assist, and what are their aspirations?
2. What fuels their passion for realizing these aspirations?
3. Does the aspiration resonate with a specific demographic, or is it universally embraced?
4. What hurdles stand in the way of turning these aspirations into reality?
5. Can you draw parallels or analogies to express your understanding of these aspirations?

Do your best to take on your audience's authentic voice, as they must believe you believe in their aspirations.

See also:
Analogy (Design by Analog, DbA) | Empathy | Maslow's Hierarchy of Needs

Calls to Action

An invitation for an audience to act.

7/100

Motivating your audience to buy a product, collaborate, or even download a document hinges on delivering a compelling call to action (CTA). User Experience (UX) designers strategically incorporate CTAs using buttons, shopping carts, and persuasive text, purposely shaping user experiences that encourage action.

A CTA might encourage an audience to seize a limited-time deal or simply sit back, relax, and enjoy the unfolding of a narrative. Some CTAs instill a fear of missing out (FOMO), while others are seamlessly woven into a story to assert control over an audience.

CTAs come in various forms, from guiding users through digital environments to navigating physical environments, like retail stores that direct shoppers to visit overlooked and under-shopped areas. I've embedded CTAs in hotels and airports to hasten the flow of guests and travelers while influencing where they might eat and shop. Even a traffic signal is a CTA, imparting critical information to drivers. The success of a CTA depends on the perceived value awaiting the audience on the other side of an action—a value that must be conveyed in your narrative.

Be careful, however, as overly aggressive CTAs may lead to disengagement, while passivity risks being overlooked. It's crucial to strike a balance. Consider what level of urgency your audience will tolerate.

Compelling CTAs demand clarity, starting with solid command verbs that eliminate ambiguity and decisively guide the audience. This clarity reduces decision fatigue and responsibility. Writing CTAs in the first person fosters trust and confidence, making your audience feel as if they are empowered and part of the action. When an audience feels a CTA was written specifically for them, they are more likely to act.

Strategic CTAs generate anticipation by providing enough information, leaving the audience eager for more details, which can be revealed post-action. It's essential to avoid cluttering your CTA with elements that detract from the primary request and subsequent value.

CTAs do not have to be associated with physical activities. Heineken and Apple used calls to action to encourage a lifestyle change. Heineken seeks to motivate humans to bond with people different than themselves, perhaps over a beer. Apple's call to action is to think differently creatively and possibly aspire to be as great as the individuals in their ads. Hulu's call to action replaces the expected "buy now" with "plan your movie night." Hulu takes the pressure off buying and puts the spotlight on what is desired.

See also:
Essence Model | Kano and Storytelling | The Peak-End Rule

Compelling CTAs demand clarity, starting with solid command verbs that eliminate ambiguity and decisively guide the audience.

Ceremonies and Rituals

The way humans practice their customs, both formally and informally.

8/100

American botanist and author Robin Wall Kimmerer says, "Ceremony focuses attention so that attention becomes intention. If you stand together and profess a thing before your community, it holds you accountable." This is evident in the design community, where we engage in multiple ceremonies and rituals, such as design critiques, stand-ups, brainstorming sessions, research, and more. The attention we pay to these ceremonies and rituals translates directly into the intentionality behind our work.

What does this have to do with storytelling? Ceremonies, rituals, and stories produce the same results. They are felt personally, resulting in physical, spiritual, and emotional bonds with other humans. Humans become agreeable when engaged in all three activities, even those who fundamentally disagree with one another. If you partake in ceremonies and rituals as a part of your design practice, embed those experiences in the stories you tell. Let your audience know how these ac-

tivities make a difference in your work. If you do not engage in ceremonies with your design team, devise one or two that represent how you bond as a team or how an element of your design process contributes to a healthy culture.

Consider the unboxing of an Apple product, which transcends mere packaging—it is a carefully designed and executed ceremony. The gradual separation of the box lid, the unveiling of the product, and the meticulous disassembly of each component create a sensory and, for some, sensual experience. Retaining Apple product boxes by a significant percentage of customers is not solely driven by resale value; it's a testament to the emotional resonance of the unboxing ceremony.

Embedding ceremonies and rituals, whether ordinary or extraordinary, within a design narrative elevates its value.

See also:
Dramaturgy | Choreography | Master Planning

Embedding ceremonies and rituals, whether ordinary or extraordinary, within a design narrative, elevates its value.

Character Relatability

An audience's ability to relate and draw a connection to characters in a story.

9/100

When you tell a story, you invite others into your narrative space. For those unfamiliar with the characters in your story, it is your responsibility to introduce attributes and peculiarities that foster connections. Those characters might include designers, consumers, stakeholders, or the design itself.

Until your audience understands the character's motivations, likes, dislikes, abilities, and failures, it will be challenging to immerse themselves in the narrative. The relationship between a character and an audience thrives when there's an acknowledgment of the character's significance to the story as well as an understanding of their distinguishing qualities. In fiction, characters move plots along and create intrigue for an audience.

In design narratives, characters do the same thing. When successful, they foster an enduring appeal. When unsuccessful, they prompt swift disengagement. The key lies in establishing relatability or the audience's ability to connect with characters meaningfully. It's crucial to note that relatability without interest and intrigue risks making a character tedious, resulting in audience disengagement. Intrigue could be achieved through foreshadowing, hinting about a character during exposition, and creating anticipation. Similarly,

interest relies on the same mechanism that keeps audiences engaged in mysteries by including a sense of urgency. This can be achieved by carefully inferring the benefits related to your design without revealing details all at once.

The following five attributes assist in creating high levels of character relatability:

1. Like all humans, characters should have flaws and vulnerabilities, which do not weaken them but make them relatable.
2. Assigning aspirations, goals, and purpose to characters humanizes them and demonstrates that they have agency.
3. Small, unexpected details, like a fearsome villain stopping for ice cream, can add depth and nuance to a character.
4. Characters can be assigned emotions and values. Whether aligned with the audience's or not, these emotions and values provide the basis for understanding the character's actions and motivations.
5. During the exposition phase, don't forget to provide a character's origin story. Explore where they came from and why they were created. Add conflicts, difficulties, and opportunities that shaped their existence.

See also:
Archetypes | Anthropomorphism | Vulnerability

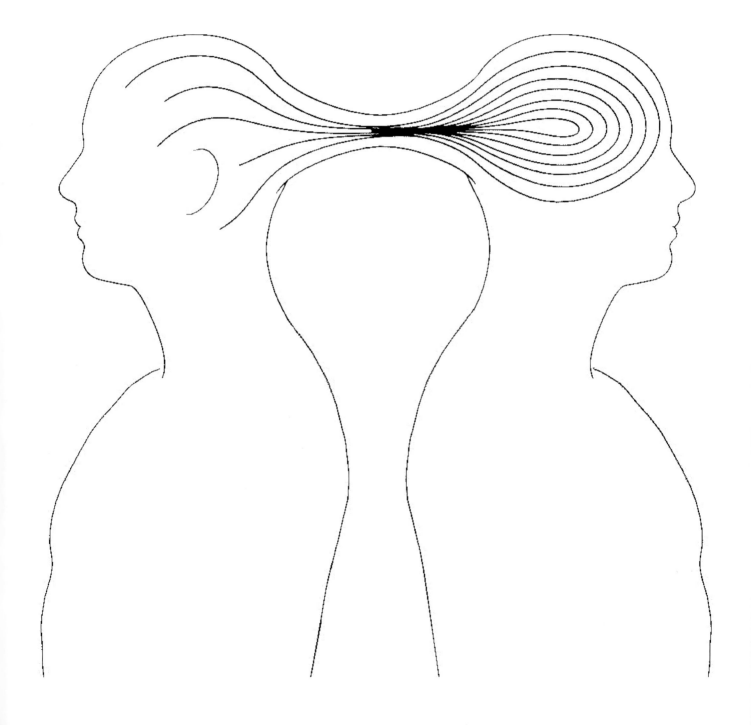

Choreography

The movement and sequencing of events, people, products, services, and experiences.

10/100

Every design incorporates components of movement or the deliberate orchestration of events that express a design's form, function, and value. Integrating them into your storytelling will vividly illustrate the design's simplicity, complexity, and impact.

User Experience (UX) choreography is like a dance. It requires precise movements, from a click to a pause as the screen elements refresh: click, drag, drop, pause, click, drag, drop, pause. These actions simulate, metaphorically speaking, dance and, most certainly, rhythm. Dancers prepare themselves by practicing, rehearsing, and strengthening. Designers do the same through prototyping, testing, and iterating.

Choreography is also a prominent contributor to the successful design of physical environments like hotels, retail stores, airports, houses of worship, and more. Embracing choreography involves understanding the preferred movements of those traversing an environment. It is also a method for purposely compelling guests to move where, when, and for how long—all of which are required for an optimal experience.

The London Underground orchestrates a remarkable display of diagrammatic choreography, skillfully arranging station sequences and train directions and how they interconnect. This well-regarded graphical narrative empowers passengers to choreograph their journeys intuitively. The map streamlines movements with the exclusive use of vertical, horizontal, and 45-degree lines. Notably, it accentuates central London stations while compressing lines and stations in more remote areas. The map unveils the potential for a synchronized dance between humans and trains. Esteemed dance choreographers, such as Bob Fosse or Martha Graham, crafted distinctive choreographies by establishing permissible and restricted movements—akin to how the London Underground precisely dictates and permits specific travel routes.

When composing your design narrative, integrate the essential user interactions and movements that lead to success. Take inspiration from the seamless flow of the London Underground, and always feel free to represent these movements graphically.

See also:
Ceremonies and Rituals | In Medias Res | Rhythm and Silence

UX choreography is like a dance. It requires precise movements from a click to a pause as the screen elements refresh:

click, drag, drop, pause, click, drag, drop, pause.

Conflict

The friction between two opposing forces.

11/100

Conflict serves as a catalyst for transformation, igniting the designer's passion for crafting solutions to human challenges. Conflict not only exists between humans but also includes the struggles between humans and places, technology, society, and nature, as long as two things disagree or oppose each other's disposition. Audiences become engaged when conflicts arise, offering a deeper insight into strengths, vulnerabilities, and motivations.

There are two primary classes of conflict: internal and external. Internal conflict occurs when opposing forces reside within a single character or entity. For instance, a character embarks on a painful internal deliberation, grappling with moral dilemmas and weighing the righteousness of their decisions. Conversely, external conflict arises from sources beyond a character's control. In such cases, he must act deliberately while recognizing that the conflict and underlying motivations originated outside of himself.

There are six fundamental types of opposing forces that generate conflict:

1. Character versus Character(s): This conflict involves complex individuals with opposing beliefs and motivations, such as heroes versus villains or Montagues versus Capulets.
2. Character versus Society: This conflict involves a character that challenges governments, organizations, or corruption, a character driven by a deep passion to overcome his opposition.
3. Character versus Nature: Conflicts with nature are often formidable, requiring persistence and creative thinking to ensure survival or adaptation.
4. Character versus Technology: Characters may conflict with technology when it malfunctions, is misused, or clashes with others who employ it for nefarious purposes.
5. Character versus The Supernatural: Confronting the supernatural involves facing the unknown, a terrifying force without prior knowledge to guide the way.
6. Character versus Self: This internal conflict revolves around moral dilemmas, where characters must carefully deliberate their choices, often depicted as the classic angel on one shoulder and devil on the other.

Conflict appeals to all humans, capturing and holding our attention until a resolution is designed.

See also:
Affect as Information Theory | Character Relatability | Jekyll and Hyde Syndrome

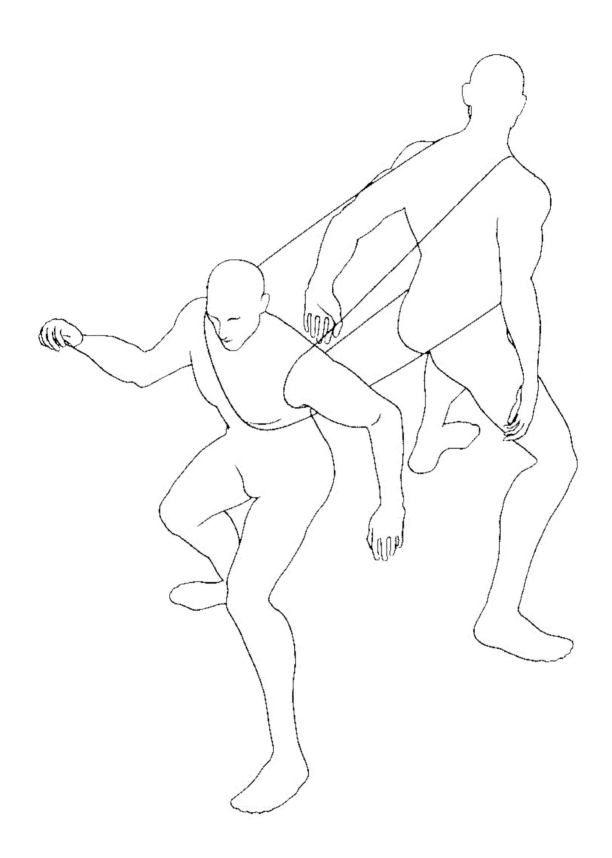

Contrast, Beginning to End

A distinct otherness must exist between the beginning and end of your story.

12/100

Stories and designs are catalysts for transformation, guiding us from familiarity and the status quo toward a new and distinct reality. In design, the status quo marks our awareness of a problem or opportunity in need of change. In storytelling, it signifies the ordinary world before it undergoes a transformation, ideally leading to improvement.

Before the start of a vacation, there is an ordinary world, a status quo. The vacationer is tired, bored at work, and stressed about family issues. Upon returning, he is relaxed, has clarity of thought, is more creative, and hits the ground running. If we do not know his state (in the ordinary world) before the vacation, it will be challenging to appreciate the effect of his time away.

Before designing a solution for a village in drought-stricken sub-Saharan Africa, suffering, disease, and little hope exist, if one is unaware of the desperation in the ordinary world, the return of freshwater will seem less impactful; the narrative will be ineffective, and fewer people will invest or provide resources. Moreover, if the story begins with the innovative filtration system instead of the existing human problem, the audience will never understand the enormity of the transformation.

The distinctiveness between a pre-transformed world and transformation must be well-defined. This distinctive otherness constitutes one of the most crucial elements of your story. Failing to portray this contrast makes it challenging to appreciate the transformation's significance and the depth, breadth, and effort required to execute impactful change.

Reflect on your portfolio of designs, and tell a very brief story about the beginning and end, leaving out everything in between.

See also:
Allegory | Proximity | Show, Don't Tell

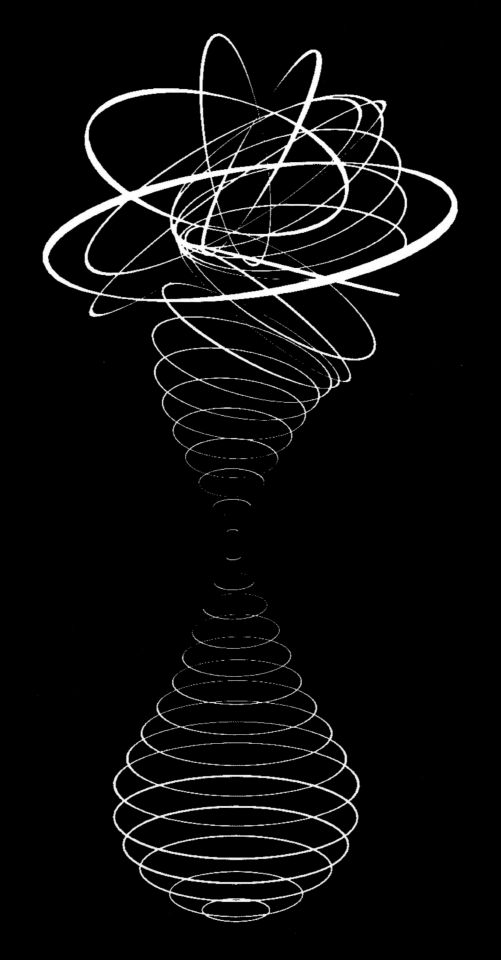

Core Values

Embedded principles and beliefs that guide actions and behaviors.

13/100

Crafting a set of core values has become essential for businesses, providing a foundational framework that encapsulates the beliefs, principles, and ideals guiding a brand. Integrating these values into a design narrative profoundly influences consumers and benefactors. Consider a design story interwoven with the core value of environmental friendliness—consumers who choose this design, consciously or subconsciously, align themselves with the commitment to sustainability. Those already embracing this core value reinforce their dedication, while those unfamiliar have the value reflected upon them.

Equally crucial is integrating core values into a design team's practice—communicating the moral principles underpinning their work and the stories they tell. This fosters strong connections with clients and consumers who share these values.

In fiction, core values help distinguish between protagonists and antagonists, symbolizing the dichotomy of good versus evil. In real life, core values might determine the willingness of a consumer to approach or avoid a design.

The essence of core values often lies in their intangible benefits and the promises they extend to consumers. They are intricately linked to emotions that shape perceptions of a design and its creators. However, authentic alignment between values and the entity they represent is crucial. Core values must genuinely motivate the entire design team and contribute to the overarching design and corporate culture.

When incorporating core values into a narrative, ensure they meet the following criteria:

1.   Show they are being lived and motivate your team.
2.   They are understandable and shareable through word of mouth and marketing.
3.   They are relatable to all audiences.

Core values are adaptable. As culture, socioeconomic conditions, technology, and environments evolve, adjusting or adopting new values may be necessary. They serve as guidelines for an organization, determining accepted work, rejected work, the type of designers hired, and clients with whom you'd prefer to work.

See also:
Essence Model | Hofstede's Cultural Dimensions Theory | Resource-Based Theory (Marketing)

Crafting a set of core values has become essential for businesses, providing a foundational framework that encapsulates the beliefs, principles, and ideals guiding a brand.

Creativity
Using one's imagination to create original ideas.

14/100

Rarely does a narrative unfold or a design materialize without an infusion of abundant creative energy. Even stories rooted in fact and driven by data require imaginative thought and careful consideration to ensure resonance with an audience.

The mere mention of creativity often elicits diverse reactions, with one common response being, "I am not a creative person." Despite some reluctance to embrace the label of being creative, the innate ability to imagine is universal. Nevertheless, for many, creative skills tend to diminish with age.

In 1968, Dr. George Land conducted a pioneering study that assessed the creativity of 1,600 children aged three to five enrolled in a Head Start program. The study utilized a test originally developed for NASA to identify innovative engineers and scientists. Upon revisiting the same group at ages ten, fifteen, and through adulthood, the findings unveiled a percentage decline in creativity levels:

- Test results among five-year-olds: 98 percent creative.
- Test results among ten-year-olds: 30 percent creative.

- Test results among fifteen-year-olds: 12 percent creative.
- The same test given to 280,000 adults: 2 percent creative.

"What we have concluded is that noncreative behavior is learned," stated Dr. George Land.

Storytelling acts as a creative catalyst for brainstorming, sparking innovation, and tapping into the collective imagination of a group. When creative atrophy takes its grip, try telling stories; it will free the imagination.

An insightful approach to creative storytelling aligns with the perspective of the US Patent Office, which underscores three fundamental elements crucial for fostering creativity.

- Originality: An idea that is novel, unusual, or independent.
- Usefulness: An idea that holds value and is likely to work, offering a solution to a problem.
- Surprise: An idea that is not obvious, providing a unique twist or surprise, even if the essence of the idea is not entirely original.

See also:
Human Technology | Music | Show, Don't Tell

Data Storytelling

Renders data into a consumable and actionable narrative.

15/100

When we break data down to its smallest unit, "datum," we find it to be one-dimensional, confined to its initial form, be it a word, image, genome, spreadsheet cell, or musical note. In this raw state, it lacks inherent meaning. So, how can we imbue data with dimension and purpose? How does it become relevant—and actionable—especially in a world where it is abundant, freely accessible, and rapidly expanding?

Relevance and dimensionality emerge when data integrates with other data, forming recognizable patterns and messages, much like musical notes on a score orchestrating a symphony. Data storytelling serves as the transformative mechanism that bridges the gap between knowledge (factual information), understanding (confidence and certainty), and wisdom (the ability to act). Data storytelling empowers the mind to efficiently navigate extensive volumes of information, unveiling concealed characteristics, patterns, anomalies, and evolving trends.

Data visualization is the primary tool that accelerates or makes a data story digestible, acting as the intermediary between data and the human mind. Users can validate their expectations and unearth the unexpected by revealing the connections between disparate data elements. In practical terms, data visualization conveys substantial structured and unstructured information across geographical and cultural boundaries. If effectively done, a data story can be expressed without verbal narratives.

The goal of data storytelling is to unlock and clarify through visual exhibits information that would otherwise remain concealed or hard to see. This does not require simplifying information. Instead, data storytelling helps make data comprehensible and actionable.

Data storytelling guidelines include:

- Identify the data's significance to your target audience.
- Assess the feasibility of conveying your story without verbal narration.
- Clearly articulate the desired actions for your audience post-engagement.
- Leverage all three axes—X, Y, and especially the Z-axis—for deeper insights.
- Incorporate context and contrast where possible.
- Exclude decorative elements or chart clutter; display only pertinent information.
- Choose colors thoughtfully.
- Simplify technical complexity for broader comprehension.

See also:
Allegory | Calls to Action | Jobs to Be Done

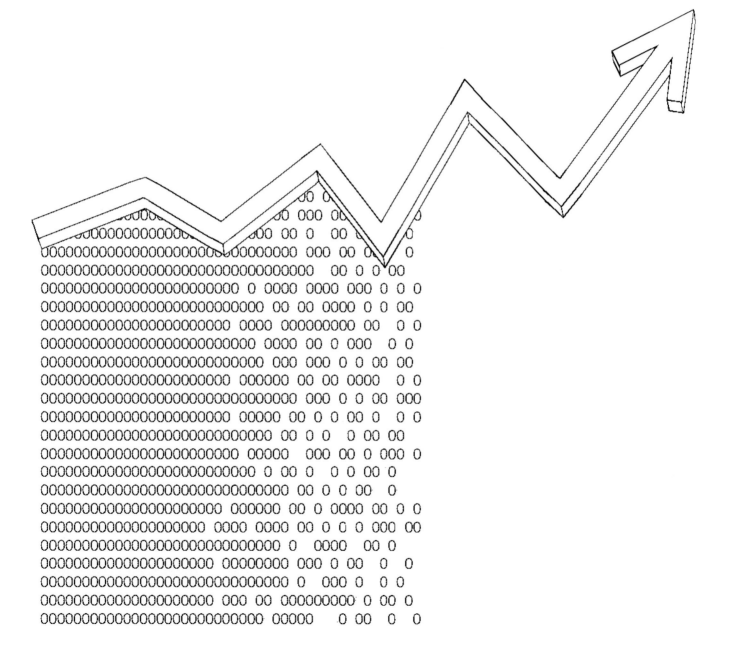

Deceptive Cadence

An effective and dramatic way of adding surprise to your story.

16/100

A deceptive cadence is a moment of surprise or a shift in tone that diverges from what one might anticipate. While it can be subtle, it typically carries a significant, even dramatic, impact. At the very least, it's unmistakable and reveals something unforeseen.

I've drawn inspiration from music. An orchestra can initially immerse its audience in a serene melody, only to suddenly transition into a powerful overture. When executed with skill, this maneuver instantly captivates the undivided attention of the audience, possibly revealing a characteristic, nuance, or aspect that had been intentionally concealed.

In storytelling, this strategy effectively alleviates audience fatigue, arouses their engagement, and encourages them to refocus and take notice. I was introduced to the concept of the deceptive cadence during a lecture by Maestro Benjamin Zander. Zander explained that composers often use this technique to "reclaim the listener's attention," a method frequently employed in horror films.

While we find comfort in predictable stories, it's the unexpected—often unsettling—that truly captivates us, creating a more memorable and enjoyable experience.

We are drawn to stories that skate on the periphery of what we anticipate.

In the movie *Carrie*, the audience is led to believe that the young protagonist has met her demise, only for her hand to emerge from the ground during the film's climactic moments. While we've become somewhat accustomed to such narrative twists, the revelation that Darth Vader is Luke's father in the *Star Wars* series was undeniably mind-blowing. Similarly, Alfred Hitchcock masterfully delays the unveiling of Norman Bates's mother in *Psycho*, initially presented as the driving force behind the story's violence, only to reveal her as a lifeless corpse, with Norman adopting her persona.

In nonfiction, I frequently employ deceptive cadence when unveiling an additional layer of value in my designs, especially as the story concludes. As I revealed the design of a tellerless retail bank—detailing the branch layout, aesthetics, customer flow, and cutting-edge technologies—I intentionally withheld the revelation of the substantial economic savings that the financial institution would realize until the very end of my narrative. The audience responded positively throughout, but the well-timed reveal of these financial benefits truly elevated the narrative.

See also:
Hitchcock's Rules of Visual Storytelling | Rhythm and Silence | Stickiness

When executed with skill, this maneuver instantly captivates the undivided attention of the audience, possibly revealing a characteristic, nuance, or aspect that had been intentionally concealed.

Deductions

The human technology that enables decision-making.

17/100

Humans go into perceiving mode when we hear stories. As we absorb the thoughts and ideas that are being shared, we begin to make decisions. We ask the following question: Is what I am hearing true or false, helpful, or not? This type of reasoning is our attempt to simplify or better understand the story being presented in order to come to a reasonable or logical conclusion. There are multiple factors that account for how we make those decisions; some include social impact, personal preference, age, and past experiences that influence future choices. The stories you tell will summon the same response: your audience's desire to make the right decisions through effective deductions.

Deductions begin with wide-ranging thoughts that are narrowed down to specific conclusions. When information is not available, incorrect deductions will be drawn. It is up to the teller of a story to offer helpful clues. For instance: *All dogs have an acute sense of smell. Fido is a dog, so Fido has a keen sense of smell.*

In this very short story, a general statement is made and examined, and a logical conclusion is drawn. To an extent, and to the best of our ability, we predict the con-

sequences of a statement or condition based on what we know; we predict what we think the observation should be if the concept is correct. However, if Fido lost her ability to smell, my answer would be different.

In the commercial world, not all information is true, no matter how convinced one might be. For instance, I stayed at a hotel that had no soap or shampoo. I would have made the following deduction: *All hotel rooms have showers. All showers come with soap. Therefore, all hotel showers have soap.* In my case, this level of deductive reasoning did not work. Given the amount of data I had at my disposal—decades of staying in hotels that provided soap in showers—one would have concluded, logically, that this hotel would have supplied soap in the shower. I was wrong, and the brand paid the price.

When crafting your story, act just as much as a storyteller as a detective; think about Sherlock Holmes and his ability to observe, process details, and make deductions. Listen carefully—out loud—to your stories, and determine if you've left out any clues that will lead to an incorrect conclusion.

See also:
Dramaturgy | Narrative Design | Show, Don't Tell

Deus ex Machina

The resolution of a hopeless or unexpected situation by a divine or miraculous power.

18/100

Deus ex machina originates from the Latin expression "God from the machine." This literary device, frequently encountered in film and theater, introduces a plot twist that offers relief within a tense narrative. Anticipated calamities take an unexpected turn toward happiness as *Deus ex machina* intervenes, injecting an element of divine surprise and resolution. When all hope is lost, *Deus ex machina* saves the day.

In classical mythology, a hero teeters on the brink of demise, facing a formidable beast. As hope wanes, a god descends from the rafters in the direst moment, defeating the creature and allowing the hero to press on with their pivotal journey. *Jurassic Park* provides a vivid instance of *Deus ex machina* when two children and their adult companions confront impending danger from velociraptors. Suddenly, without explanation, a T-Rex materializes mysteriously, swooping in to rescue them and enabling them to make a narrow escape. This narrative device resonates deeply with humanity's penchant for triumphant resolutions as we vicariously immerse ourselves in the struggles and perils of characters yearning for deliverance.

The phenomenon extends beyond fiction into real-life anecdotes. I vividly recall a fire erupting on my college campus just before a final for which I was unprepared—an unforeseen but welcomed miracle. Similarly, a moment of financial desperation turned fortuitous when a twenty-dollar bill lay unexpectedly on the floor beside me. Instances of narrowly avoiding calamities, like oversleeping and missing a flight that later crashes, add layers to these tales. While grounded in fortuitous timing, these stories captivate us with their improbable outcomes. Despite criticism from literary experts for being an easy way out of a difficult situation, *Deus ex machina* undeniably delivers emotionally gratifying resolutions.

Translating this concept to the world of design, one can leverage *Deus ex machina* as a storytelling device to showcase the resolution of a complex or wicked problem through creative design ingenuity. The more wicked the problem, the closer the designer resembles the god lowered from the rafters, unraveling an ostensibly insurmountable issue. Crafting a compelling narrative involves vividly describing an affliction, followed by the strategic actions taken by the designer to unearth a solution. While the resolution may not match the dramatic flair of a T-Rex saving the day, the allure lies in presenting seemingly miraculous resolutions.

See also:
Conflict | Dramaturgy | The Hero's Journey

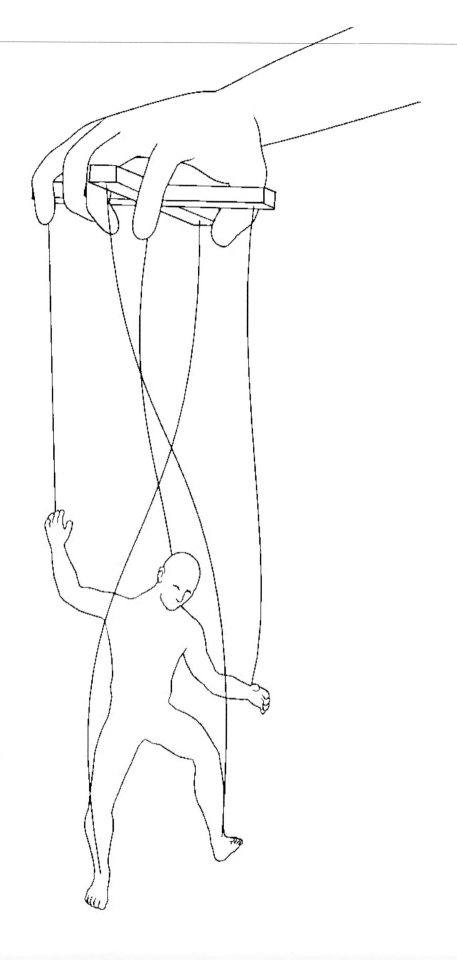

Dieter Rams' Principles of Design

Ten principles for good design and great storytelling.

19/100

Dieter Rams, the iconic industrial designer, laid down what I like to call "design commandments"—a set of principles that serve as a beacon for exceptional design. When woven into your narratives, these principles illuminate a well-balanced and globally aware story.

1. Good design is innovative. Technological development always offers new opportunities for original designs. But imaginative design always develops in tandem with improving technology and can never be an end in and of itself.
2. Good design makes a product useful. A product is bought to be used. It has to satisfy not only functional but also psychological and aesthetic criteria. Good design emphasizes the usefulness of a product while disregarding anything that could detract from it.
3. Good design is aesthetic. The aesthetic quality of a product is integral to its usefulness because products we use every day affect our person and our well-being. But only well-executed objects can be beautiful.
4. Good design makes a product understandable. It clarifies the product's structure. Better still, it can make the product talk. At best, it is self-explanatory.
5. Good design is unobtrusive. Products fulfilling a purpose are like tools. They are neither decorative objects nor works of art. Therefore, their design should be both neutral and restrained to leave room for the user's self-expression.
6. Good design is honest. It does not make a product more innovative, powerful, or valuable than it really is. It does not attempt to manipulate the consumer with promises that cannot be kept.
7. Good design is long-lasting. It avoids being fashionable and, therefore, never appears antiquated. Unlike fashionable design, it lasts many years—even in today's throwaway society.
8. Good design is thorough down to the last detail. Nothing must be arbitrary or left to chance. Care and accuracy in the design process show respect toward the user.
9. Good design is environmentally friendly. Design makes an important contribution to the preservation of the environment. It conserves resources and minimizes physical and visual pollution throughout the lifecycle of the product.
10. Good design is as little design as possible. Less, but better—because it concentrates on the essential aspects, and the products are not burdened with non-essentials.

See also:
Ceremonies and Rituals | Core Values | Ethics

Good design is as little design as possible. Less, but better — because it concentrates on the essential aspects, and the products are not burdened with non-essentials.

Disney's Twelve Basic Principles of Animation

Fundamental principles of animated storytelling and character design.

20/100

Disney's legendary group of original animators, known as the Nine Old Men, played a pivotal role in shaping some of the most timeless animated tales such as *Snow White*, *Cinderella*, and *Sleeping Beauty*. Among these visionaries, Ollie Johnston and Frank Thomas detailed twelve principles of animation, as illustrated in their seminal book, *The Illusion of Life: Disney Animation*.

These principles, now fundamental in the world of animated storytelling, extend their influence beyond traditional and computer-generated animation to UI, CSS, and even PowerPoint presentations, breathing life into designs, narratives, and presentations.

For example: **"Squash and Stretch"** illustrates the impact of gravity on characters through expansion and compression, lending a natural fluidity to their movements. **"Anticipation"** sets the stage for forthcoming events, capturing moments like a hero inhaling before a daring leap or an athlete gearing up for a decisive ~~throw or~~ kick. Meanwhile, **"Staging"** demands that every movement or pose conveys clear intention, ensuring the audience's focus remains unwavering in a scene.

"Straight Ahead and Pose to Pose" offers a distinct approach. "Straight Ahead" involves drawing frames successively, while "Pose to Pose" crafts a character's movements as the story unfolds, starting with key poses and filling in the in-between motion later.

"Follow Through and Overlapping Action" simulates the laws of physics and inertia, depicting scenarios where a character halts, but various body parts stop at different times. **"Slow-in and Slow-out"** mirrors real world movement dynamics, demanding gradual acceleration and deceleration for authenticity.

"Arc" replicates natural movement along arched paths, mimicking realistic motion—like the graceful turn of a character's head. **"Secondary Action"** promotes complementary movements that enhance primary actions, such as a character running with their hair flowing in the wind as a secondary action.

"Timing" empowers animators to manipulate time by adjusting frame count, reflecting the weight and response of objects or characters to stimuli. **"Exaggeration"** injects emphasis into movement without sacrificing believability, often adding a touch of humor.

"Solid Drawing" insists on a 3D appearance for all elements, even in 2D animation, suggesting the inclusion of animated drop shadows for a minimal sense of depth. Lastly, **"Appeal"** centers on a character or object's charisma and personality, fostering audience empathy and engagement.

See also:
Character Relatability | Mise en Scène | Rhythm and Silence

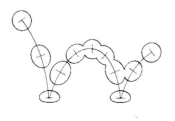

Squash and Stretch

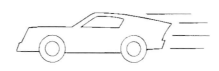

Timing and Motion

Anticipation

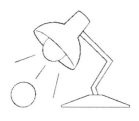

Staging

Follow Through
and Overlapping Action

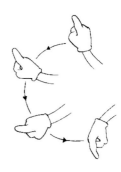

Straight Ahead and
Pose-to-Pose Action

Arcs

Slow In and Out

Exaggeration

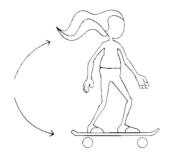

Secondary Action

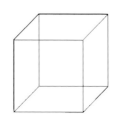

Solid Drawing

Appeal

Dramaturgy
The theory and practice of dramatic composition.

21/100

Dramaturgy is to theater as design thinking is to design.

Dramaturgy is the adaptation of a narrative into a performable structure, not unlike transitioning a design from concept to execution through design thinking. Both seek the same thing: relevance for the audience who sees a theatrical production or the consumer who is enticed by a design.

There are two fundamental parallels between design and dramaturgy. The first revolves around thorough research, while the second centers on rigorous testing. Just as a design researcher delves into understanding user needs, a dramaturge aims to ensure a play connects with its audience. Meanwhile, designers conduct research to define the user experience (UX) comprehensively. In a theatrical production with archaic language, the dramaturge facilitates comprehension for actors and directors, ensuring the meaning of unfamiliar dialogue is conveyed effectively. Similarly, in design, complex technical properties must be simplified.

A dramaturge will consider the experience from the moment an audience enters the theater just as a designer will consider every aspect of a design (the total UX), from initial awareness to purchase, unboxing through the usage of a product.

Dramaturgy and design are interested in what sociologist Erving Goffman called impression management, or how to control other people's impressions through sign vehicles, signifying how they would like to be identified. While there are numerous sign vehicles, Goffman most frequently alluded to the following:

Settings serve as the physical or virtual backdrop for a performance or experience. Whether it's an office, a screen, a restaurant, or a virtual meeting, it plays a crucial role in shaping the atmosphere of the interaction while influencing the narrative.

Appearance refers to the outward physical appearance of an individual or design. This includes what we wear and how we hold ourselves. Appearance is a sign vehicle that will be noticed and evaluated, perhaps associated with an archetype that compliments or conflicts with a brand's intention.

Manners of interacting are typically nonverbal gestures, facial expressions, and body language. Manners project an attitude or a sign for humans to approach, avoid, or advance cautiously.

What sign vehicles do you consider during the design and storytelling process, and how can sign vehicles influence the stories you tell?

See also:
Archetypes | Choreography | Mise en Scène

Emotion
The instinctive responses to external stimuli.

22/100

The designer and storyteller share a common goal: to arouse emotions in others. An individual who is emotionally affected by stimuli (a story or design) goes through a chemical process, a physiological state that is formed subconsciously. This occurs due to the presence and elevation of dopamine, serotonin, norepinephrine, and endorphins.

These chemicals are released throughout our bodies based on external triggers or instantaneous reactions to stimuli. Simply put, one has an emotion—an inner, indispensable, and familiar sensation that manifests in a feeling that prompts an action or behavior.

Emotion is an extremely powerful influencer. However, knowing how every human will emotionally respond to stimuli is impossible; therefore, examining our own responses to stimuli and empathizing with your audience is crucial. When effective, emotions spawn greater audience engagement, higher memory retention, and a greater likelihood that your design story will be shared with others.

Several steps can be taken to ensure you are touching the right emotions in your design story:

- Determine the emotion you hope to touch in your audience, and ensure they resonate culturally, ethically, and demographically (test on multiple humans).
- An emotion can quickly lead to a behavior or action, so always include a call to action, assuring that emotions do not override actions.
- Share your own emotional experience, and allow yourself to be or seem vulnerable.
- Conflict arouses the attention and emotions of others because humans relate to the strengths and weaknesses of others.
- The more vivid and descriptive your words, images, and sensory details are, the more likely you will strike an emotional chord in your audience.
- Human transformation always arouses emotion.
- Be aware of the role of each emotion and understand its powerful impact on the humans you serve, and never make anyone feel they are being emotionally manipulated.

See also:
Affect as Information Theory | Calls to Action | Empathy

The more vivid and descriptive your words, images, and sensory details are, the more likely you will strike an emotional chord in your audience.

Empathy
The ability to understand the feelings and needs of others.

23/100

If an individual understands their own character, feelings, biases, motives, and desires, they are self-aware. Equally important is the awareness of other humans and their life experiences, sitting in the domain of empathy. Whether you subscribe to the evidence-based techniques of human-centered design or not, empathy is always a factor in design and storytelling.

When we are empathetic, we learn what makes people tick. It is easy to collect demographic data, and with a little digging we could gather psychographic data, revealing personality traits, values, attitudes, interests, and lifestyles. While this data is very useful, it is only data and there is a big difference between knowing and understanding. The act of empathy draws one closer to understanding the complex, expressed or latent needs of the humans you serve. Knowing, or knowledge, is based on the discovery or recall of data. It implies a level of expertise, experience, and education. It provides a level of certainty. Understanding, on the other hand, entails an in-depth consideration of the connections between humans and moments of time, resulting in a deeper level of meaning. Understanding is "guttural." It's an essential step that allows us to put knowledge to better use. With each observable moment of humans being, a new level of understanding emerges which leads to empathy, a natural and inbred human technology. An interesting anecdote is said to have come from a class anthropologist Margaret Mead was teaching.

A student asked Margaret Mead what she considered the first sign of civilization to be in culture. The anticipated answer was a tool of some sort of artifact that had a connection to faith or religion. However, Mead's answer was a 115,000-year-old fractured femur bone. She explained that the femur bone is the longest bone in the human body. It links the hip to the knee. If broken, it could take up to 8 weeks to heal properly. The discovered bone was clearly broken and subsequently healed. In the animal kingdom, Mead clarified, a broken bone, such as the femur, ends poorly—in death. There is no ability to run from prey, hunt or heal peacefully. That unfortunate animal is no longer the hunter but rather the hunted. This 15,000-year-old healed femur bone provides evidence that the wounded person was cared for by another person and given the proper time to recover. This bone suggests that one human helped another rather than desert them, and in that act risked their own life, proving that empathy is an organic human trait. Empathy is a critical tool that assures us that we are designing relevant, valuable, and approachable experiences.

See also:
Emotion | Phenomenology | Show, Don't Tell

With each observable moment of humans being, a new level of understanding emerges which leads to empathy, a natural and inbred human technology.

Epigraph

A brief phrase, quotation, or poem that acts as a preface to a story.

24/100

An epigraph is a short saying, quotation, or summary placed at the beginning of a book, chapter, or presentation. One might include an epigraph to expose an inspiration, to set the tone or theme of a story, to help an audience become prepared for what is to come. I insert epigraphs, typically in the form of a quote, as an expository element breathing life into my story or design. For instance, in my attempt to get an audience to better align with a design concept, I began with this quote by Steve Jobs: "Design is not just what it looks like and feels like. Design is how it works." This was the perfect epigraph that warned the audience that we would talk about mechanics and function. I spoke the quote and inserted it into the "leave behind" material. It is permissible to insert various epigraphs throughout the telling of a story, adding gravitas, clarity, and credibility.

The nice thing about an epigraph is that you don't need to write it, you only need to find it. The epigraph you select does not have to be directly linked to your design or story. For instance, a story related to service design in a hospital does not require an epigraph on healthcare or service design. It could very well be a quote on the power of human transformation and desire to innovate. While the underlying theme might be hospital service design, the epigraph warns the audience that the topic is about change.

Do not use an epigraph as a substitute for exposition; in many cases, the epigraph serves as an introduction or curtain opener for exposition. If the connection to your epigraph is not made clear until later in a story, it is always a good idea to inform your audience. Only use an epigraph if it serves a purpose. While I have collected hundreds of great quotes, I always check their quality, cultural references, and purpose before I use them.

See also:
Plot | Sensemaking | Rhythm and Silence

The nice thing about an epigraph is that you don't need to write it, you only need to find it.

Essence Model

Essence is the basic nature of a thing— the quality or qualities that make a thing what it is.

25/100

Contemplate the full scope of an object, location, individual, or narrative that you are reasonably familiar with. When its defining attributes and traits are readily discernible, its essence becomes apparent. An essence model serves as the framework for conveying something or someone's fundamental nature.

The following four qualities define an essence model:

1. The way something can be described or recognized. A golden retriever has four paws, golden fur, and a long tail. These attributes contribute to its essence, the things that make the dog what it is. Moreover, these physical and observable attributes are factual and indisputable.
2. What does something or someone do (intent)? A dog is a family companion or locates illegal contraband at the airport. How something is offered, consumed, or serviced influences its essence.
3. How does something make one appear (external)? Do I believe the essence of something makes me appear more independent, intelligent, or cre-

ative? That perception, real or not, contributes to the essence of something.
4. How something makes one feel (internal). You cannot discuss essence unless it extends to how someone or something makes you feel. For example, does the essence of something make you feel more confident, feminine, masculine, taller, or prouder? I might understand something is black or white, but how the color makes me feel is vital to its essence.

Essence transforms ideas into stories and designs into experiences, forming a deeper connection with your audience. An essence model could be used in two ways: by embedding these qualities during exposition or by revealing each quality throughout your story as new information is provided or transformation occurs.

How many attributes or characteristics of an essence model can be removed before its essence is no longer familiar?

See also:
Archetypes | Mary's Room | The Willing Suspension of Disbelief and Poetic Faith

Ethics

The standards that express what is right and what is wrong.

26/100

I grappled with the decision to delve into the topic of ethics, mindful of avoiding a didactic tone that suggests straying from these principles makes you subpar. The aim is far from condemnation; the ten considerations below will elevate designers and storytellers to a moral high ground. They form a holistic guide, urging designers and storytellers to create with empathy, transparency, and a profound understanding of their work's impact on the world.

1. Usability:
    • Will your design and story be easy to understand, and will your audience learn something new?
2. Efficiency:
    • Does your design enhance productivity with minimal effort and waste?
3. Safety:
    • Will your design and story create a sense of well-being for users and listeners?
4. Accessibility:
    • Does your design and story cater to individuals with diverse abilities and disabilities?
5. Transparency:
    • Are the features and value of your design and story transparent to your audience?
6. Avoid Excessive Persuasion:
    • Respect your audience's autonomy by avoiding excessive persuasion.
7. Beware of Bad Actors:
    • Ensure that your work does not become a tool for nefarious purposes.
8. Understand the Impact:
    • Consider the lives led by those who adopt your design or become influenced by your story.
9. Environmental Impact:
    • Assess the potential environmental repercussions of your design and story.
10. Captivate Hearts and Minds:
    • Does your design or story possess the qualities of pleasantness, delight, interest, and agreeability?

See also:
Hofstede's Cultural Dimensions Theory | Maslow's Hierarchy of Needs | Vulnerability

The ten considerations below will elevate designers and storytellers to a moral high ground.

Exposition
An introduction to a story's critical background information.

27/100

Exposition acquaints an audience with essential background details, including characters, locations, props, materials, and the overarching tone and tenor of a narrative. It imparts just enough information to establish an emotional and cognitive connection between the audience and the story. The absence of exposition may lead to misguided assumptions about a story's theme, resulting in confusion and disengagement.

Achieving a delicate balance is essential—too much expositional information breeds apathy, while too few details leave audiences adrift, forcing them to fill in the gaps themselves. Exposition should gracefully lead an audience into a story rather than bombarding them with a list of facts, features, and functions.

There are several forms of exposition, including:

1. Description/definition: Identifying the uniqueness of elements within the design/story, its objective, the job it is expected to do.
2. Comparisons: Highlighting similarities between two or more entities, setting context by drawing parallels with other designs and stories.
3. Contrast: Emphasizing differences between entities, illustrating how your design deviates from other familiar designs.
4. Cause and effect: Unveiling the problem your design seeks to solve and the transformational effect of its solution.
5. Classification: Organizing entities based on shared characteristics and sorting those items into discernable categories.

Consider including these items in your expository writing.

- Introduce any locations relevant to the usage of the design.
- Familiarize your audience with any support players integral to the design.
- If technology is an enabler, let it be known.
- Offer just enough foreshadowing to reveal what might be unexpected but with no big spoilers.

One of the most renowned and impactful methods of exposition can be seen in the opening crawl of the *Star Wars* epic. Following the crawl's completion, the audience is primed for the unfolding narrative. This method was first used in 1940 for the opening sequence of *Flash Gordon Conquers the Universe*.

Some of the best examples of nonfiction exposition can be read in cookbooks that offer anecdotes describing the meaning, familial, or historical importance of the recipe and any cultural or geographical information that prepares and excites the reader.

See also:
Contrast, Beginning to End | Foreshadowing | Tone and Tenor

Exposition should gracefully lead an audience into a story rather than bombarding them with a list of facts, features, and functions.

Foreshadowing
A warning or indication that something is about to happen.

28/100

Foreshadowing serves as a fundamental technique, subtly hinting at future developments, thereby shaping the narrative's trajectory and plot. In design narratives, foreshadowing takes on a pivotal role in unveiling the benefits and broad applicability of the design.

Foreshadowing is often used as an element of exposition, alluding to situations on the horizon. In fiction, especially in film and television, this technique is often called "planting and payoff," where information is subtly exposed (planted) only for the payoff to be revealed later in the story. One of the best examples of this principle is in the film *Citizen Kane*, where Charles Foster Kane's dying word, Rosebud, is spoken at the beginning of the film. It is not until the film's end that the audience learns that Rosebud is Kane's childhood sled.

In the past, I have foreshadowed the scalability, usability, ROI, and innovation associated with a design, only to reveal details later in my narrative. The one thing to remember is that foreshadowing should not spoil a revelation; it provides a clue that something important is coming while inserting a level of suspense.

There are two distinct types of foreshadowing:

- Direct foreshadowing provides a clear, explicit, and purposeful exposure to something that will happen.

- Indirect foreshadowing is far more subtle and might come in the form of hints spread throughout a story.

In fiction, foreshadowing can be expressed directly through dialogue or character. In nonfiction, it is revealed by a subject matter expert. I've heard foreshadowing presented as a question that asks an audience to consider upcoming events with an answer to follow. The title of a story could provide enough foreshadowing to captivate an audience.

When using foreshadowing in your design stories, strategically plan where to situate your direct and indirect clues. The sooner you reveal those clues, the more effective and long-lasting they will be. Feel free to distribute your hints, but make sure the most critical clues are near the beginning.

Foreshadowing could be used as a red herring to mislead or distract an audience, only for the unveiling to be a welcome surprise.

One could also use prolepsis, a literary device that involves disrupting the chronological order of events within a story by presenting a future plot point earlier in the narrative than its actual occurrence.

See also:
Deceptive Cadence | Exposition | Meaning versus Value

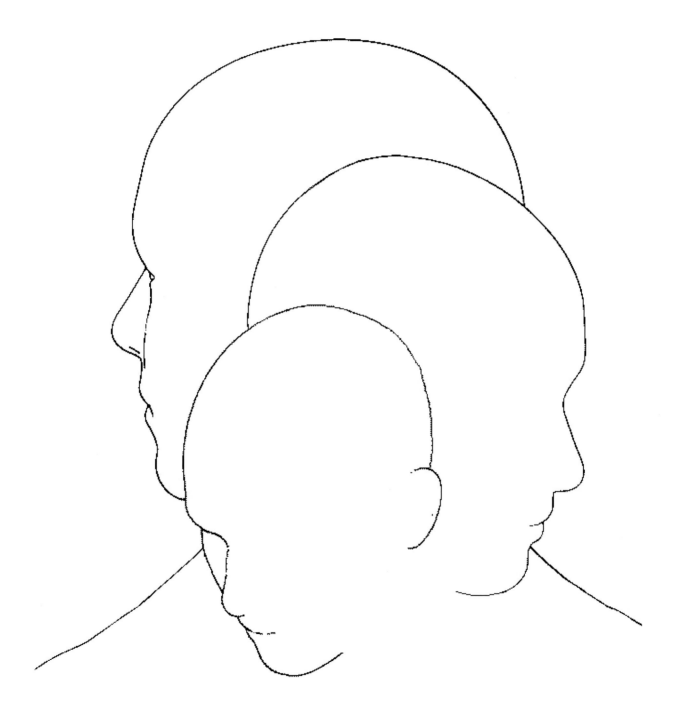

Form and Function
Appearance and utility must be in balance.

29/100

When constructing a design narrative, embracing various principles is crucial, among which lies a cornerstone: the interplay of form and function. Form represents the design's outer visual and sensory character, while function embodies its purpose and practical utility.

I've offered a nuanced alternative in past design narratives by substituting form and function with aesthetics and mechanics. These two elements are inseparable, constituting a symbiotic relationship that demands equilibrium for optimal impact. A design's emotional or subjective allure must be balanced with its objective utility to resonate effectively.

The common pitfall lies in disjointed descriptions, where the sensory and emotional appeal—the design's form—is extolled without explaining the design's purpose, reliability, and user-friendliness, giving rise to uncertainty. The questions linger: "Does it look appealing but also perform effectively and with enduring reliability?" Conversely, a design solely focused on functionality may address a problem but may risk being dismissed as aesthetically deficient and unappealing. Without a balanced narrative, a design may appear either overly intricate and monotonous or captivating yet devoid of substance.

To ensure equilibrium in your design narrative, consider the following key elements:

1. **Define Purpose:** Clearly articulate the purpose of the design. While you need not delve into the intricacies of each function, it is paramount to have clarity regarding the design's intent.
2. **User Experience:** Illuminate the user's journey through the design, intertwining emotional nuances with practical usability concerns. At each stage of the journey, reveal how the design's form was meticulously developed to resonate with the identified user base.
3. **Contextual Relevance:** Acknowledge the context of your narrative. Tailor your emphasis on form or function based on the target audience. Engineers evaluating design viability may prioritize functionality over aesthetics, while luxury car shoppers might initially focus on visual appeal rather than technical details.
4. **Function must always precede form!**

A discerning storyteller emphasizes the mutual influence of form and function, illustrating that a well-balanced narrative reveals subjective and objective dimensions.

See also:
Core Values | Essence Model | Jobs to Be Done

A design's emotional or subjective allure must be balanced with its objective utility to resonate effectively.

Freytag's Pyramid
A multistage guide to dramatic structure.

30/100

Freytag's Pyramid, conceived by Gustav Freytag in 1863, is a structural framework for narratives. It draws inspiration from Aristotle's *Poetics* that coalesced plot structure into three parts: the introduction, the crisis, and the catastrophe or resolution. Freytag, a German novelist and playwright, contemporized Aristotle's structure with his pyramid.

This framework is designed to engage audiences, fostering empathy for the characters and subject matter—offering a deeper understanding of their complex issues. By adhering to Freytag's guidelines for dramatic structure, audiences are more likely to suspend their disbelief. This framework extends beyond fiction; Freytag's Pyramid has provided valuable guidance for various marketing strategies, enhancing the success of products and services. This structure offers a coherent, linear progression that logically links one stage of a story to the next. It unfolds as follows:

- **Exposition:** This initial stage introduces the audience to the story's setting, time, characters, and location. It provides just enough information to acquaint the audience with the story's world and hints at impending conflicts.
- **Rising Action:** This stage reveals the core conflict, often triggered by an inciting incident, also known as the rising movement. It may involve the protagonist uncovering the antagonist's sinister motivations, presenting hurdles and obstacles that forewarn impending trouble.
- **Climax:** The climax is the pivotal juncture of the story, representing the turning point and often the most dramatic phase. The characters' destinies are either unveiled or foreshadowed, creating an emotional peak in the narrative.
- **Falling Action:** This phase unveils the resolution or aftermath of the climax. It typically encompasses the resolution of conflicts between antagonists and protagonists or the resolution of problems presented during the inciting incident. However, the drama may not be entirely over, as additional elements of suspense may be included.
- **Denouement:** Often referred to as the resolution, conclusion, or "moment of catastrophe," this is the story's conclusion. It could result in a positive or negative outcome, as long as it resolves the initial problem, conflict, or battle. With this conclusion, the audience should experience a sense of catharsis or emotional release.

Stories that fail to evoke catharsis, should examine the steps of Freytag's Pyramid and determine which element is conspicuously absent from the narrative structure.

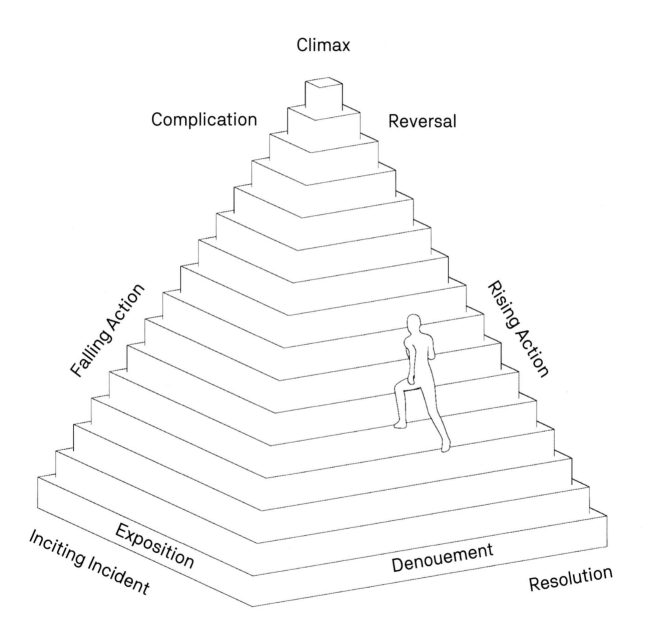

Climax

Complication

Reversal

Falling Action

Rising Action

Exposition

Inciting Incident

Denouement

Resolution

Functions of Storytelling
The multiple functions and forms of storytelling.

31/100

The response to once upon a time is clear.

We know what happens next.

We pause and pay attention.

We prepare to engage in a relationship with the teller of a story and the story that follows.

Depending on the teller and the nature of the story, we are filled with fear, delight, or fright.

We, humans, are perpetual storytellers and listeners.

We tell stories to be entertained.

We tell stories to share our collective experiences.

We tell stories to the young, preparing them to take their place in the world and perhaps make it better.

We tell stories to teach and learn.

We tell stories as a tool for survival, so we know when to fight or flee.

We tell stories to promote and maintain our traditions, rights, rituals, and ceremonies.

We tell stories to explain our first-person experiences, hoping to gain empathy or sympathy.

And we tell stories to influence other humans to see things our way, buy things they need or don't need, or plant ideas and touch them emotionally—to get them to feel, understand, and act.

Stories are told based on how we dress, what we eat, how we behave, the way we move, and with whom we associate.

Stories also live within us, privately and quietly. They are our internal narratives, helping us make decisions and solve problems. These stories do not take the form of verbal or symbolic expression; they remain in our minds until adequate meaning, value, and motivation inspire us to share with others.

All of these stories are born of the inspirations and stirrings of their creator. And, of course, creators are inspired by the needs and desires of the humans who benefit by paying attention to stories told.

Gestalt

The whole of something is greater than the sum of its parts.

32/100

The human mind naturally perceives objects, experiences, brands, or products as unified wholes rather than isolated parts, a concept rooted in gestalt psychology. This theory, pioneered by Max Wertheimer, Kurt Koffka, and Wolfgang Köhler, suggests that our response to stimuli is shaped by how various elements come together to form a cohesive whole.

In design, every component serves a distinct purpose to contribute to the overall form and function. Humans instinctively grasp the complete picture before discerning individual elements—a principle captured by the famous phrase, "The whole is greater than the sum of its parts." This holistic perception extends to storytelling, where the entirety of the narrative holds more significance than any isolated passage.

Max Wertheimer's Law of Prägnanz, or "good figure," underscores the perceptual and affective association of stimuli to create a coherent gestalt. It emphasizes simplicity, asserting that objects or stimuli are perceived most straightforwardly, as our minds naturally fill gaps to simplify complexity.

Gestalt theory encompasses 7 fundamental principles:

1. Closure: The mind fills in missing parts to construct a complete entity.
2. Similarity: Similar elements are naturally grouped based on shape, color, or size, regardless of proximity.
3. Continuation: Our perception follows the smoothest path of a line.
4. Proximity: Elements closer to each other or overlapping are perceived as having a stronger relationship.
5. Symmetry and Order: Also known as Prägnanz, it relates to how our brains interpret shapes most simply.
6. Common Fate: Objects moving or pointing in the same direction are grouped together.
7. Figure-Ground: Our brains differentiate between the foreground (figure) of something and the background it sits upon.

Gestalt principles offer a crucial framework for designers, influencing aesthetics, functionality, and user-friendliness. Once internalized, these principles become apparent in daily observations, enhancing your design sensibility as well as providing clues to crafting compelling stories.

See also:
Conflict | Form and Function | Proximity

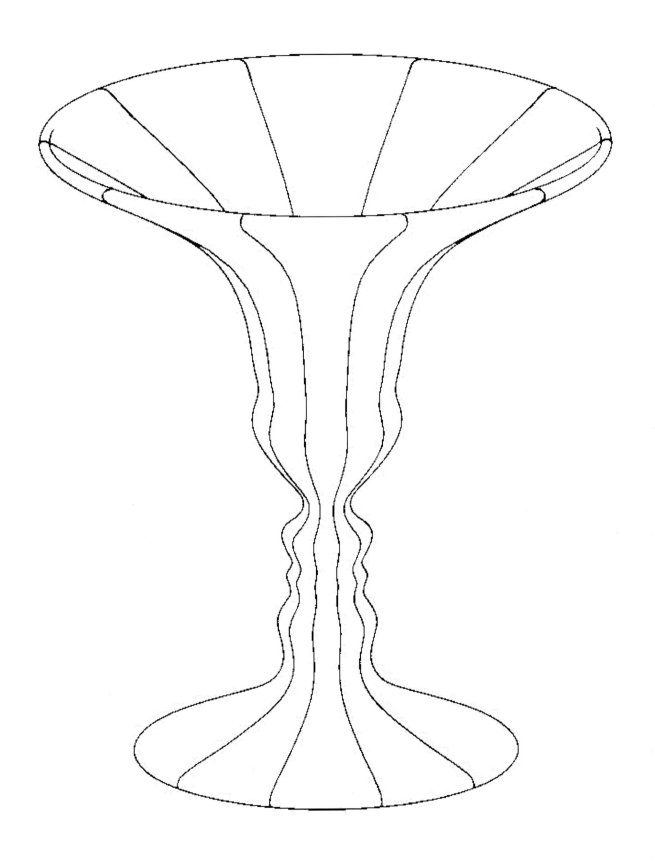

Happily Ever After
The end of a story, assuming stories ever end.

33/100

While we cannot predict the future with certainty, we understand that life is dynamic and ever evolving. Stories, being reflections of our lives, naturally undergo transformations. The concept of "happily ever after" is merely a moment in time when our past experiences shape what lies ahead. As beings endowed with agency, creativity, and technical prowess, we possess a unique ability to invent our future and craft narratives that provide glimpses into our evolution.

For designers and storytellers, "happily ever after" extends beyond the conclusion of a tale or the completion of a design narrative. Take, for instance, the story of *Beauty and the Beast*. In its "happily ever after," the Beast transforms into a Prince, marries Belle, and the enchanted characters return to their human forms. While this might seem like the end of the story, life persists. The narrative continues with passion, children, challenges, prosperity, war, peace, celebrations, and mourning. Although a story's explicit words, images,

and actions may conclude, its essence endures. This realization is a potent tool for storytellers and designers alike, prompting us to envision how a design unfolds beyond its initial purpose.

For designers, it involves contemplating how a product, service, or experience will be used and perceived over time. When does its relevance peak? How long before it requires an update or improvement? What are the human needs that occur after "happily ever after"? This creative endeavor should motivate designers to innovate, enhance, consider what will be, and become authors of ever-evolving stories, emphasizing that the narrative we craft shapes the future we desire.

Considering this "after happily ever after" prompt: Is my design or story as comprehensive and enriched as possible, and what happens after it is delivered and used? Take one of your existing design stories and add a chapter that projects its future—be wildly creative.

See also:
Creativity | Jobs to Be Done | Theodore Levitt and the Quarter Inch Hole

Is my design or story as comprehensive and enriched as possible, and what happens after it is delivered and used?

Hitchcock's Rules of Visual Storytelling

Three rules to live by when telling visual stories.

34/100

Rule One: Start with a sweeping establishing shot or statement to set the scene. This instantly orients your audience, providing context before introducing the characters and other expository elements.

Rule Two: Direct the audience, not the actors. Director Alfred Hitchcock's approach favored visual storytelling over excessive dialogue. Shoot every scene, and use imagery with the audience's perspective in mind, using the camera as their eyes. This technique empowers you to control emotions and engage viewers on a higher emotional level.

Rule Three: Size matters in the frame. Objects' significance should match their size at any given moment. This complements rule two by directing the audience's focus. When a character or element is crucial, go for an extreme close-up or prominence to emphasize its importance.

Direct the audience, not the actors.

Hofstede's Cultural Dimensions Theory

A guide to cultural similarities and differences.

35/100

Gerard Hendrik "Geert" Hofstede, a Dutch social psychologist, formulated a theory to gauge and comprehend cultural dimensions within diverse regions and organizations. This theory delves into how culture shapes the values embraced by its members and explores the correlation between these values and the subsequent behaviors.

Hofstede's Cultural Dimensions Theory comprises six dimensions:

1. **Power Distance Index (PDI):**
   - High PDI indicates a hierarchical culture where authority goes unchallenged and is revered.
   - Low PDI signifies an egalitarian culture that values equal, democratic, and informal ways of working and behaving.
2. **Individualism versus Collectivism (IDV):**
   - Individualistic cultures prioritize personal goals and achievements, embracing autonomous working.
   - Collectivist cultures emphasize group work, consensus, and collaboration, often communicating indirectly.
3. **Masculinity versus Femininity (MAS):**
   - Masculine cultures are competitive and assertive, valuing direct communication.
   - Feminine cultures prioritize cooperation, empa-

thy, quality of life, relationships, and equality.
4. **Uncertainty Avoidance Index (UAI):**
   - High UAI cultures seek stability, structure, and predictability, expecting adherence to process and rules.
   - Low UAI cultures tolerate flexibility, embracing creativity and openness to new ideas.
5. **Long-Term versus Short-Term Normative Orientation:**
   - Long-term-oriented cultures are pragmatic, thrifty, and patient, requiring negotiation and cooperation.
   - Short-term-oriented cultures focus on the present, seeking immediate outcomes and feedback, and are often less inclined toward compromise.
6. **Indulgence versus Restraint (IVR):**
   - Indulgent cultures prioritize personal gratification, accepting personal opinions, emotions, and fun.
   - Restrained cultures emphasize self-control, discipline, and strict behavior, often reflecting reserved and distrustful traits.

Utilize these six dimensions to discern the appropriate and acceptable manner to craft your designs and stories. While the world is becoming more interconnected, recognizing distinct cultural norms remains an imperative.

See also:
Contrast | Core Values | Ethics

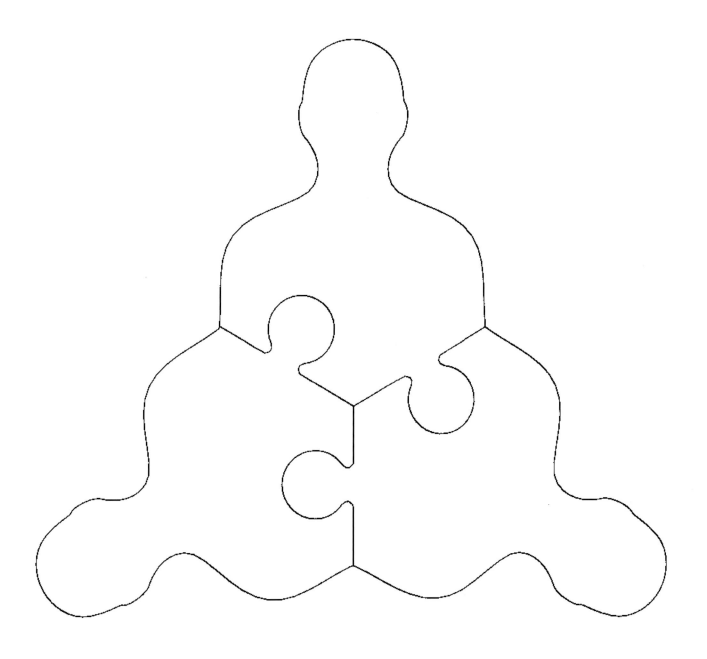

In essence, each culture may respond uniquely to a design or narrative.

Human Technology

Our inborn abilities that allow us to function organically.

36/100

As beings of the *Homo sapiens* brand, we have several superpowers, or innate human technologies, that allow us to navigate the world successfully. They include:

- Our advanced cognitive ability: we are very good at acquiring knowledge and making sense of our everyday life.
- Our articulate speech: we communicate clearly—or at least attempt to—in multiple languages and manners.
- Our ability to stand upright: cool maneuver when you think about the stick-like appendages that keep us aloft.

Observing and decoding the features and functions of human technology provides clues for how we work and how we play, as well as insights into our limitations, our controls, and our proficiencies, all the information required to design the things humans need and desire.

For the most part, humans do well "unaugmented" without the help of built technologies. However, when human technologies are damaged or become less effective, we design ways to compensate for and augment our natural abilities. While other species transform involuntarily to survive environmental or physical challenges (or become extinct), we design, tell stories about our designs, and pass them on to future generations who improve upon them.

So why talk about human technology? When we tell stories about our designs, which almost always includes elements of manufactured technology, we often forget to consider the human technology that enables us to use the inorganic technology successfully. The three examples above—cognition, speech, and movement—provide a starting point. These extend to our five senses that help us make sense of the world and avoid danger. In your design stories, for every technology mentioned, it is highly recommended to highlight the human technology that will be used as an enabler.

See also:
Choreography | Observing | Stimulus, Organism, Response Theory

While other species transform involuntarily to survive environmental or physical challenges (or become extinct), we design, tell stories about our designs, and pass them on to future generations who improve upon them.

Hyperbole
Exaggerating the mundane.

37/100

To be hyperbolic is to exaggerate but without being taken literally. The word is derived from the Greek *huperbolē,* meaning "thrown above."

Picture someone declaring, "I am so hungry I could eat a horse." While the hunger is genuine, the prospect of devouring a horse is purely hyperbolic. Yet, those around the hungry individual instantly grasp the intensity of the hunger, influencing the choice of a dining venue. Humans use hyperbole to offer a high degree of clarity, and, when well executed, it introduces a slice of humor.

Hyperbole transforms the mundane elements of your story into crystal clear portrayals, overstating the understated that might otherwise be ignored or quickly forgotten. Hyperbole increases memorability and the likelihood that your primary audience will spread the theme of your story by repeating those memorable hyperbolic statements to others. The key to successful hyperbole is to be sure it is not taken seriously or literally. After all, an individual with normal cognitive abilities would not believe me when I say I am so hungry I could eat a horse.

I use hyperbole to amplify elements of a design. For instance, "The color is so bright it is like looking at the sun." Or, "Sleeping on that bed is like sleeping on a cloud." Or, "The new first-class seat will make you wish the flight never ends." I've heard this hyperbole used a million times by those fortunate enough to sit in an exclusive first-class cabin.....well, I've never actually known anyone to do anything a million times. Still, the hyperbolic statement makes a defining point.

Hyperbole should move your plot forward, emphasize a point, or clarify an element of your design that requires emphasis. Hyperbole is challenging to write; even the Beatles had to work "Eight Days a Week" to conjure their hyperbolic statement.

See also:
Deceptive Cadence | Metaphors | Show, Don't Tell

"I am so hungry I could eat a horse."

While the hunger is genuine, the prospect of devouring a horse is purely hyperbolic.

In Medias Res
A story that begins in the middle, not the beginning.

38/100

If you ever joined a conversation or story in progress, you have experienced *in medias res*, literally translated from Latin as "into the middle of things." Despite its drawback of bypassing traditional exposition, theme, or inciting incident, *in medias res* is a dynamic way to captivate attention by plunging an audience into the heart of the action. This method, ultimately, circles back to a story's origin, gradually unveiling knowingly omitted-yet-crucial information.

Opting for an *in medias res* narrative style transforms the storyteller into a puzzle master. In doing so, you become the architect of anticipation and excitement, a technique often employed in genres like police dramas or film noir, where the tale commences with a gripping incident and then unravels backward to reveal essential exposition.

This narrative method serves a dual purpose. First, it establishes an atmospheric mood early on, sidestepping a prolonged introduction and allowing the audience to immediately dive into the story's intrigue. Second, it creates a sense of mystery and anticipation.

Rather than starting a design narrative by introducing the design team, research, or problem that requires a solution, you might start by sharing a prototype or a video testimony of an individual who has benefitted from the design. I've witnessed this technique used by a design firm specializing in medical devices. The presentation began with a short video of a young patient after her life-saving operation. She seems strong, hopeful, energetic, and very likable.

Of course, the story eventually flashed backward to the critical nature of her condition, technical information, and how the design team worked with surgeons to create, test, and manufacture the lifesaving device. This instance of *in medias res* created a heightened emotional response.

The success of *in medias res* hinges on meticulous planning. Before constructing this narrative puzzle, plot all necessary details. This strategic groundwork ensures you don't inadvertently omit crucial elements. Begin the narrative at a critical juncture, but hint that events of significance will transpire before and after. Adopt a single narrator's voice: Similar to film noir, speaking through one voice will provide cohesion and clarity.

Using *in medias res* ensures your audience will remain firmly tethered during your unfolding tale. If a more traditional method fails, try this unorthodox approach.

See also:
Deceptive Cadence | Foreshadowing | The Paradox of Suspense

Begin the narrative at a critical juncture, but hint that events of significance will transpire before and after.

Infrathin
A feeling so small it is barely perceptible.

39/100

There is a sense, an experience, that is not a sense at all; it's not even a word found in the dictionary, a word without a definition but unquestionably a feeling: IN-FRATHIN. You cannot touch it. You might not be able to explain it, but you feel it. The term was coined by French artist Marcel Duchamp, who sought to disturb rigid thinking and introduce provocative dialogue in the arts. He was famous for what was referred to as "readymades"–everyday objects he transformed into art by selecting, modifying, and presenting them in new ways. They included a wooden stool with a bicycle wheel attached to it and a urinal named "Fountain." Readymades were Duchamp's way of becoming free of a specific style or taste; in his words, they were the "trap" many artists fell into.

Infrathin's mission is to remain difficult to define or attach a name to the gap between creating an object and the created object, the inexpressible elements of creativity itself. Language could not describe the intersection where we have an internal, visceral reaction to something, only more profound, but we do not quite understand how it could be explained. Consider the difference between two seemingly identical objects, like two liquids, and the variance between how they feel. The difference could be minute or figuratively immeasurable and unexplainable.

I am borrowing the concept of infrathin as a worthy and discoverable asset that helps to define the about-ness of a design, brand, or story. Today, consumers find indistinguishable characteristics from product to product, surpassing the ability to recognize the differences. Most recently, as I walked the main street of a small beach community, I observed no less than six coffee shops and three fast-food taco stalls. It was impossible to distinguish what made them unique. The only distinguishing factor might have been their infrathin. Infrathin experiences include:

- The warmth of a seat just after another person got up.
- The moment ice melts in a glass of water.
- The imprint of a sock around an ankle after the sock is removed.
- The connection two people feel through the static electric cling.
- The "whish" of a revolving door.

What infrathin have you experienced? What occupies that hard-to-define space that contributes to the aboutness of your design story, the thing that makes a human being feel? What are the moments that exist but are hard to define or describe? They draw your attention and contribute to the essence that becomes embedded in memory and that are called upon when a decision needs to be made about what coffee shop or taco stand to visit.

See also:
Phenomenology

You can not touch it. You might not be able to explain it, but you feel it.

Jekyll and Hyde Syndrome

Two distinctly different characteristics residing in the same organism.

40/100

"Jekyll and Hyde" has found its way into popular culture to describe markedly different characteristics or behaviors within a single organism. Anyone who has had a lousy waiter in a seemingly reputable restaurant could bear witness to this type of duality. Dr. Jekyll and Mr. Hyde are no different than stories that provide little-to-no synchronization across communication channels.

It has become imperative for businesses to leverage as many channels and modes of communication as possible, essentially doing whatever it takes to grab and hold the attention of humans. Common (but mistaken) theories suggest that the more channels used, the more exposure one gets (more opportunities to sell). Owning multiple channels requires the management and curation of multiple personalities. If those personalities do not harmonize, the results will be harmful. The most devastating consequence is the "Jekyll and Hyde syndrome"— one purely approachable characteristic linked to one purely unapproachable characteristic attached to a single entity. It causes brand confusion, doubts about quality, lack of authenticity, and ambiguity on the part of humans (consumers). If I met Dr. Jekyll, I would likely have a positive impression of a virtuous man. If, however, I came across the evil antagonist, Mr.

Hyde (same guy), I would be struck by the inconsistency of the same organism.

Cognitive dissonance occurs when beliefs, ideas, and values contradict an experience, causing mental discomfort and confusion. In a commercial environment, lack of consistency and contradiction puts undue responsibility and pressure on the human (consumer). If that human cannot reduce the stress, they will abandon their interest in a brand, story, or design.

This occurs because humans naturally seek psychological consistency to survive their everyday lives or, at a minimum, lead a friction-free life. The more inconsistencies within their beliefs, ideas, and values, the more difficult it is to live productive and fulfilling lives. Humans do have the ability to justify inconsistencies as a way to diminish dissonance efficiently. One could change one's belief system to better cope with inconsistencies. However, that forces cognitive cycles on humans, who should never have been exposed to these conflicts in the first place.

Are there inconsistencies across the multiple channels that serve as your storytelling network?

See also:
Archetypes | Conflict | The Trigger

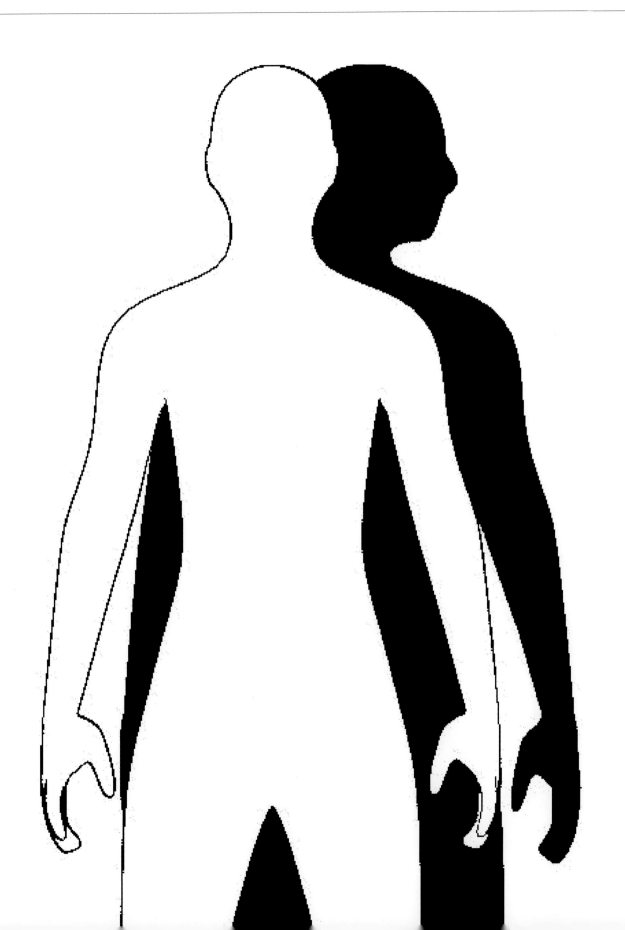

Jobs to Be Done

A schema that offers a perspective on why people buy or hire products, services, and experiences.

41/100

Jobs to Be Done (JTBD) is a compelling concept that asserts people don't simply purchase products or services; they hire them to fulfill specific needs.

JTBD pinpoints the primary purpose for which a design will be hired (purchased). This idea originated from the theories of the Austrian economist Joseph Schumpeter and his notion of creative destruction, which explains how innovation replaces outdated offerings by better understanding why people opt for new solutions. Instead of fixating on the product itself, the focus shifts to understanding and articulating the essential process, value, and task that a person seeks to achieve or experience, which informs innovations. For example, trains replaced horses because people wanted and needed to get to their destinations quickly and efficiently, and planes replaced trains for the same reason.

The contemporary concept of JTBD gained further prominence when economist Clayton Christensen introduced the term in his book, *The Innovator's Solution*. Just as we wouldn't hire an unqualified job candidate, why should we hire the wrong product, service, or experience? Addressing this question offers immediate clarity, leading to a brief and indispensable narrative.

Understanding the core job a design is intended to fulfill clarifies the narrative and humanizes the design.

The following statements lead to a comprehensive JTBD statement.

1. "I need to" = the consumer's needs, impulses, and rationale.
2. "When/where" = contextualizing the job.
3. "So that" = desired outcome.
4. "Without" = limitations or restrictions (at least limited in conditions).

Further factors include the primary tasks at hand, any secondary responsibility of the job, and the emotional or subjective responses anticipated from the interaction between the consumers and what they are hiring (your design).

JTBD defines the why behind the what. If constructed effectively and verified through user research, it provides guidance for growth and innovation. The result is a message of clarity and focus.

See also:
Analogy (Design by Analogy, DbA) | Essence Model | Kano and Storytelling

A compelling concept that asserts people don't simply purchase products or services; they hire them to fulfill specific needs.

Kano and Storytelling

Determines the correlation between product features and customer satisfaction.

42/100

Dr. Noriaki Kano, a Japanese educator renowned for his expertise in quality management, introduced this model that intricately connects design elements with customer satisfaction. The Kano Model dives deep into analyzing customer responses to various product attributes. I employ this model to enhance my designs and to understand what resonates with customers and as a blueprint for crafting compelling narratives.

The Kano Model presents five distinct categories that shape product development not solely from a technical viewpoint, like manufacturing machine components or coding websites, but from a human-centric perspective that prioritizes expectations and how offerings perform. These five classifications are as follows:

1. **Basics:** These encompass qualities and features that customers expect or consider fundamental—they are "must-haves." While their fulfillment doesn't typically result in high satisfaction levels, their absence is sorely felt, often leading to negative feedback. For instance, the absence of a bed in a hotel room would yield a poor basic story.
2. **Performance Characteristics:** These attributes directly correlate with the level of investment in an experience and the resulting satisfaction. They are features that customers evaluate compared to alternatives, often from the competition. Stories of performance highlight aspects like improved gas mileage, softer leather, or enhanced taste.
3. **WOW or Excitement:** These elements are always appreciated but not obligatory. Their absence does not reduce satisfaction as long as the basics and performance aspects are well-executed. When present, WOW elements can elevate value into meaningful experiences. People love sharing WOW stories, such as a hotel leaving warm chocolate chip cookies, a tall glass of cold milk, and a handwritten note from the manager in the room.
4. **Indifference:** This category pertains to features and functions that neither boost nor diminish satisfaction. Mentioning these in a story can lead to indifference, apathy, and uncertainty. It's a caution against promoting or making promises about things that hold little to no value.
5. **Reverse:** Reverse represents the opposite of a desirable human response. It embodies pure negativity and should be avoided at all costs, requiring swift rectification. These are the stories of total catastrophes that generate the least favorable narratives.

Are you constructing a basic, performance, or WOW story (or a progression of all three)?

See also:
Essence Model | Form and Function | Narrative Intelligence

When present, wow elements can elevate value into meaningful experiences, differentiating and fostering long-lasting emotional connections.

Kill Your Darlings

The willing removal of content and features that do not support the value of your story or design.

43/100

"Whenever you feel an impulse to perpetrate a piece of exceptionally fine writing, obey it—whole-heartedly—and delete it before sending your manuscript to press. Murder your darlings."

Sir Arthur Quiller-Couch

Sir Arthur Thomas Quiller-Couch, revered under the pseudonym Q, distinguished himself not merely as a prolific novelist but also a luminary in the world of literature. Although this quote originated from Sir Arthur Quiller-Couch, it has been attributed to many other writers, including William Faulkner, Oscar Wilde, and Stephen King.

What designer or writer hasn't fervently bonded with a sentence, color, phrase, word, material, or nuance that was painstakingly crafted over countless hours? This principle is drawn from the world of literature but is equally relevant to design, emphasizing the importance of mercilessly eliminating elements that are ultimately unnecessary in your work. Acknowledge when cherished elements detract from rather than enhance your story or design.

I have never met a designer or storyteller who found it easy to eliminate one of their "little darlings," me included.

Here are several ways to spot little darlings:

- Seek out areas where you might be repetitive or redundant. If you've said it once, kill it unless it requires exaggeration.
- Keep your eye open for anything that is overly playful, impish, or humorous but does not move your story along or improve the quality and value of your design.
- Have you included too many features in your design story? Keep what is primary or fundamental to your story but consider eliminating secondary or tertiary features.
- If killing one of your darlings is too painful, it is probably very personal and subjective. Ask someone else to commit the murder for you.

One last suggestion: Before crafting your story, draft an inventory of elements you believe must be in your story (like features, descriptors, and personas), which ones stand out against competitive designs, and which features will WOW your audience. Include them in that order, and eliminate everything else.

See also:
Form and Function | Gestalt | Kano and Storytelling

What designer or writer hasn't fervently bonded with a sentence, color, phrase, word, material, or nuance that was painstakingly crafted over countless hours?

Kishōtenketsu

A classical narrative structure originating from Chinese, Korean, and Japanese cultures.

44/100

Nearly every story structure used in the West revolves around conflict, typically introduced early in the story, resulting in some level of transformation. This twist on story structure offers an alternative.

Kishōtenketsu is Japanese but closely aligns with *qǐ chéng zhuǎn hé* from China, where this structure originated. It is referred to as *gi seung jeon gyeol* in Korea. They all subscribe to a four-act structure that does not necessitate conflict, something Western audiences are not accustomed to.

For purposes of this principle, we'll focus on *kishōtenketsu*. This story structure is told in four acts.

- *Ki*: Introduction
- *Shō*: Development
- *Ten*: Twist (complication)
- *Ketsu*: Conclusion (reconciliation)

Ki, act one, introduces the story, characters, and theme. Act two (*shō*) explains the story's theme and characters in more detail, including the relationship between characters and how they fit in the story world. The story's structure attempts to build an emotional connection with the character, theme, and audience. Act three or (*ten*) introduces a twist or complication. This

act does not refer to the typical Western plot twist; it presents an unexpected incident not hinted at in acts one and two. Act four, the final act (*ketsu*), brings the story to an end by revealing how the consequences of act three tie together with acts one and two. The difference between the ending of *kishōtenketsu* and typical Western story structures is that characters do not need to demonstrate growth or transformation; the story only needs to show the outcome of the twist.

In the context of design stories, I have used the *kishōtenketsu* structure less to introduce a problem or conflict that requires a designer's skill. Instead, I have used this structure to present a design team, designer, or portfolio to a client. I make the initial introduction (*ki*), followed by enough detail that demonstrates value (*shō*), and then a twist (*ten*). The twist could be a unique challenge or unexpected change in events, which could amount to a piece of research that required the team to adopt a new working methodology or tool. A twist could be an internal epiphany experienced by one of the designers that led to a more effective design or conclusion (*ketsu*).

Many examples of *kishōtenketsu* can be experienced in the world of anime.

See also:
Contrast, Beginning to End | Narrative Transportation

Kishōtenketsu
Four-Part Story Structure

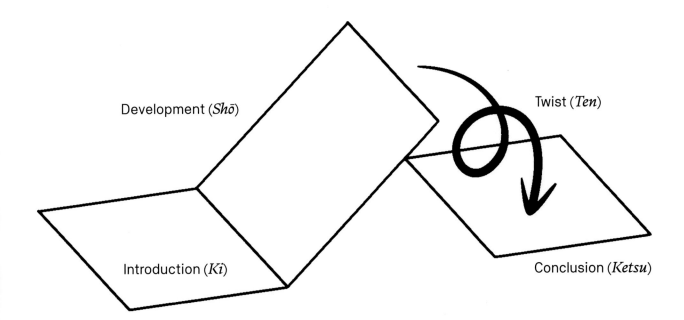

Development (*Shō*)

Twist (*Ten*)

Introduction (*Ki*)

Conclusion (*Ketsu*)

Lexicon
An upscale way of saying a list of words.

45/100

For every design narrative I craft, I curate a distinct lexicon. This is an upmarket way of saying a list of words that best describe a design and are relatable to my audience.

Consider the humble sandwich. It might be referred to as a sub—unless you are from Philadelphia, where it is a hoagie. In New York, it would be a hero, a grinder in New England, a torta in Mexico, or a panini in Italy. Despite these regional nuances, each term conjures the same culinary image. Yet, when woven into a narrative, the choice of lexicon can drastically alter its essence and impact.

Establishing a shared language fosters cohesive communication, ensuring team members are aligned in effectively addressing an audience. When crafting this lexicon, it's imperative to consider the audience's demographics, psychographics, and everyday experiences.

I've learned firsthand the pitfalls of employing terminology without a shared lexicon. On one occasion, I mistakenly referred to "cement" instead of "concrete" during a construction site visit, causing confusion over these distinct materials. Similarly, in a meeting with engineers, a colleague referred to "beams" as "columns," sparking a clarifying discussion on their respective orientations.

So, how should a lexicon be utilized? Integrate it into your daily practices, whether crafting narratives or designing products, services, or experiences. By consistently referencing your lexicon, it becomes embedded into an organization's collective consciousness, ensuring that communication with each audience feels natural. Whether in review meetings, marketing calls, scrum sessions, client interactions, or marketing materials, your lexicon becomes integral to your communication and storytelling strategy.

See also:
Core Values | Empathy | Hyperbole

By consistently referencing your lexicon, it becomes embedded into an organization's collective consciousness, ensuring that communication with each audience feels natural.

Mary's Room

An intriguing and important thought experiment.

46/100

A thought experiment is a conceptual hypothesis, theory, or principle put forward to explore and contemplate its potential outcomes and impacts.

Australian philosopher Frank Jackson devised a famous thought experiment known as Mary's Room.

Envisage a room that is black and white, void of color. A woman named Mary lives in that room. Mary has never seen color. Ironically, Mary is considered one of the leading global experts on color. She knows the physical properties of color, how humans distinguish among the millions of colors with which they come in contact, as well as the emotional impact of color. One day, Mary is permitted to leave her room, where she sees a red apple for the first time. The question in this thought experiment is, does Mary learn anything new? Does exposure to this red apple teach her anything she does not already know?

Mary's room illustrates what philosophers call the knowledge argument, where nonphysical properties and knowledge can only be fully realized through conscious experiences. This notion challenges the theory of physicalism, which posits that all mental states have physical explanations. If physicalism were true, it would suggest that Mary learns nothing new when she experiences color for the first time. Can the whole truth about an experience or object be understood without the benefit of a conscious experience?

Consider a scenario where I listen attentively as someone vividly describes their emotions—being lovestruck, tired, or angry. While I may empathize and genuinely comprehend their verbal account, can I truly feel their feelings? Philosophers refer to this subjective property as qualia—the firsthand experience of a mental state. Some argue that extensive knowledge, akin to Mary's, can provide an equivalent experience without direct sensory encounters. Conversely, others posit that true understanding necessitates subjective, conscious engagement with the subject matter.

The relevance of this debate for designers lies in our engagement with the world of experience. The narratives we craft must encompass the description of physical properties and the inclusion of qualia—the subjective sensory experiences that evoke genuine feelings. I believe that comprehensive understanding requires a conscious experience.

As you construct your design narratives, contemplate the dichotomy between knowing and feeling, using Mary's Room as a lens to explore this complex relationship.

See also:
Emotion | Resource-Based Theory | Phenomenology

Maslow's Hierarchy of Need
Five fundamental levels of human need.

47/100

In his seminal 1943 paper "A Theory of Human Motivation," American psychologist Abraham Maslow introduced a framework—the Hierarchy of Need—comprising five core needs that influence human behavior, motivation, and decision-making. According to Maslow, this Hierarchy delineates the prioritization of human needs. Conveniently, it also correlates to design and informs design narratives. Let's delve into Maslow's theory: Beginning at the base are our **physiological needs**, encompassing essentials like food, water, shelter, reproduction, and sleep—all crucial for human survival.

Ascending the Hierarchy, we encounter **safety needs**, entailing a secure environment, a source of income, protection from crime or violence, and good health.

Love and belonging follow, involving relationships with friends and family, the exchange of affection, social engagement, and intimacy.

Esteem, positioned at a higher level, encapsulates ego-driven needs, self-respect, respect from others, dignity, status, and reputation.

At the pinnacle is **self-actualization**, where individuals achieve a realistic understanding of themselves, their reality, and their purpose. This level includes education, creativity, empathy for others, motivation, and curiosity.

Maslow categorized the bottom four needs as *deficiency needs*, whose neglect leads to adverse consequences. Conversely, self-actualization resides in *growth needs*, contributing to a more fulfilling and pleasant existence without adverse effects when unmet.

Maslow's Hierarchy aligns closely with design, revealing useful parallels:

Physiological Needs: Essential functionality.

Safety: Reliable performance and trustworthiness.

Love and Belonging: Being valuable, usable, and attractive.

Esteem: Empowering people to accomplish their goals.

Self-Actualization: Realizing personal growth, satisfaction, and full potential.

Drawing inspiration from Maslow's hierarchy can be impactful in crafting a design narrative. By aligning your design goals with the motivations and desires of your target audience, you can effectively communicate how your design caters to the audience's specific levels of need.

Whether attributing a design to a single level or illustrating the dynamic movement across its continuum, utilizing Maslow's framework provides a comprehensive lens for articulating human journeys, from survival to personal fulfillment.

I recommend visually mapping your design(s) on a blank pyramid to discern its placement(s) on Maslow's hierarchy and articulate its role in addressing human needs. If your design spans multiple levels, confidently claim its dynamic alignment with Maslow's continuum of needs.

See also:
Essence Model | Hofstede's Cultural Dimensions Theory | Thesis + Antithesis = Synthesis

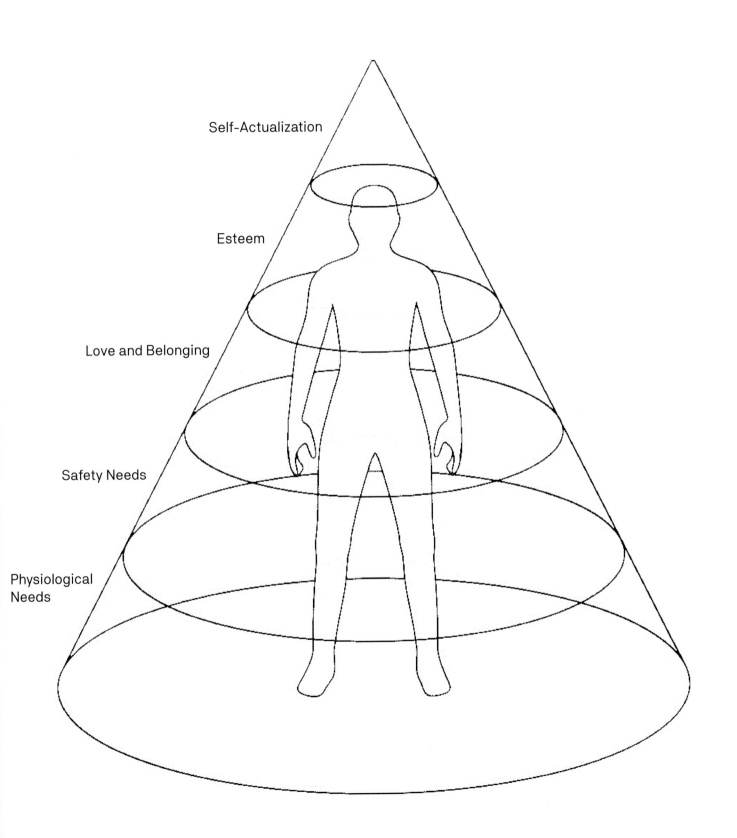

Master Planning
Every city is a story.

48/100

For just a moment, envision the cities that hold a special place in your heart. These are cities that remain vivid in your memory. They might find their way into your daydreams. No doubt, a return visit would be welcome, and you'd likely shared stories of your experiences with others, encouraging them to visit. Alternatively, consider a city you'd like to see based on the stories you've heard. You probably became aware of great shopping, restaurants, culture or theater, a renowned place of worship, a university with ivy-strewn walls and ancient bridges, not to mention parks and beaches for relaxing.

The size of a city doesn't matter. The benefits associated with a master-planned city could be found in New York, Rome, Tokyo, London, and Paris, as well as Bath, New Brunswick, and Kyoto. Master planning, in this context, lives as an inventory of features or designs that exist in the world's greatest cities, towns, and hamlets. Prominent cities share six key features inherent in their designs, each contributing to their narratives. They include structures, transportation, trade, health/safety, economic potential, layout, aesthetics, and infrastructure. Each feature provides a symbolic element of what humans deem valuable in the places they visit or call their homes. How many of the following six features apply to your design, and how would you include them in your stories?

1. An agora: a place to shop or acquire something of value. Ask: Do we have a conspicuous place to purchase or acquire something? How does that purchase get transacted, and are humans talking about and visiting your agora?
2. A park: a place to rest and reset. Ask: Is there a place to breathe and catch one's physical or cognitive breath? Is there a place to sit? Is there enough white space between the glut of information?
3. A basilica/temple: a place to worship, admire, and reflect. Ask: Does the brand promote trust and dedication, or is it simply a mark that symbolizes trade? Would one visit if he did not need to buy?
4. A university or school: a place to learn. Ask: Have you taken the time to educate or become educated? Do you learn from your brand advocates? Are the humans who buy your offering experts? Do they buy with conviction? All great cities have institutions of higher learning. Think about Apple's Genius Bar.
5. An amphitheater: a place to gather and tell stories. Ask: Is there a collaborative place to gather, listen to stories, understand culture, and provide feedback (live or virtual) (think Zoom)?
6. Neighborhoods: a group of zones with specific intent and expressed value. Ask: Are all environments, real or virtual, pixels or print, well-organized and easy to navigate?

See also:
Ceremonies and Rituals | Essence Model | Master Planning

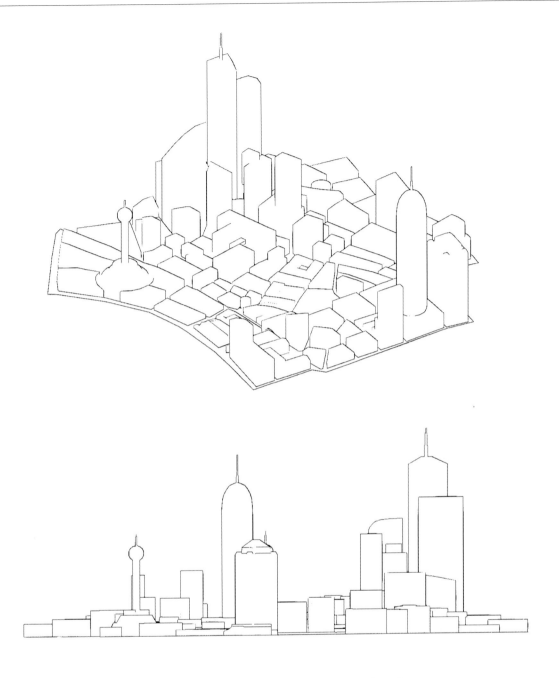

Master planning, in this context, lives as an inventory of features or designs that exist in the world's greatest cities, towns, and hamlets.

Meaning versus Value

Every story should include elements of meaning, value, or both.

49/100

The essence of a story, product, service, or experience is profoundly shaped by its meaning and value. In this context, value is a quantifiable metric, whereas meaning is a symbolic, personal, and emotional dimension.

Consider, for example, an old Timex watch passed down from a grandfather to a grandchild. While its monetary value may be minimal, the watch carries immeasurable personal and emotional meaning.

When a narrative incorporates both value and meaning, there exists a potential for one to overshadow the other, potentially leading to cognitive dissonance. This can create discomfort for the audience due to conflicting messages.

Does the core of something shift when it predominantly emphasizes either value or meaning? An audience might take offense if a story portrays an experience with an attached value when it is perceived as priceless. Designers should effectively communicate the intent of their stories, whether emphasizing value, meaning, or a balance of both, as long as these elements remain in harmony and do not contradict each other.

In 2013, Apple released a commercial titled "Misunderstood." The narrative revolves around a family coming together for their annual Christmas celebration. The central character, a teenage boy, appears disconnected as the rest of the family engages in cooking, snowball fights, and tree decorating. Unbeknownst to the family, the teenage protagonist is capturing these moments with his iPhone, a fact only revealed toward the end of the commercial when he shares the footage with his family. The family is deeply moved by the boy's creativity, realizing that the beautiful celebration has been immortalized thanks to Apple's technology. This commercial evokes a strong emotional response and is highly recommended.

The Apple narrative prioritizes meaning over value, encompassing symbolism, personal connections, and emotional resonance. Not once during this commercial is cost or function mentioned.

While value can be universally measured and agreed upon, meaning is subjective. It is challenging to fully grasp the emotional state of every consumer interested in your design, but understanding the general emotional intelligence of your target audience will significantly influence the tone of your story.

Why does this matter in the realm of storytelling? Because it is essential to strike a balance between meaning and value in your narratives.

See also:
Character Relatability | Narrative Intelligence | Theodore Levitt and the Quarter-Inch Hole

While value can be universally measured and agreed upon, meaning is subjective.

Mentalese
Our innermost narratives.

50/100

Mentalese, often referred to as the *language of thought hypothesis* (LOTH), centers around the thoughts and stories that reside in our minds. This is the rawest form of "story thinking" possible. When those innermost thoughts need to be communicated, they undergo a transformation into a language comprehensible to others. The fundamental premise is that our thoughts precede and exist separately from language.

Cognitive psychologist and psycholinguist Steven Pinker offers the following in his book, *The Language Instinct:*

> "Think about it. We have all had the experience of uttering or writing a sentence, then stopping and realizing that it wasn't exactly what we meant to say. To have that feeling, there has to be a 'what we meant to say' that is different from what we said." He goes on to say: "Many creative people insist that in their most inspired moments they think not in words but in mental images."

This is the connection to design, creativity, and innovation because it underscores our experience of navigating profound ideation before the imposition of language.

This mental landscape retains a pristine and uninfluenced quality in how we think and create as it escapes the constraints that languages impose upon us. Expressing ideas in specific languages, like English, French, or Chinese, necessitates using particular symbols, letters, and structures, dampening the spontaneity of creative thought. I have observed moments of hesitation between creativity and linguistic articulation, often resulting in a less satisfactory expression.

Pinker states: "There are far more concepts than there are words, and listeners must always charitably fill in what the speaker leaves unsaid." This insight extends the concept of mentalese to those on the receiving end of a narrative. As listeners absorb a story, they, too, have the ability to operate in their own internal language of thought, perhaps building upon the story or concept that will eventually find expression in language.

The core message regarding mentalese is that designers should attentively heed their pre-linguistic thoughts, avoiding the stifling influence of language on ingenious creative ideas. These nascent creative thoughts, residing at the precipice of expression, deserve to emerge unencumbered.

See also:
Analogy (Design by Analogy, DbA) | Hyperbole | Lexico

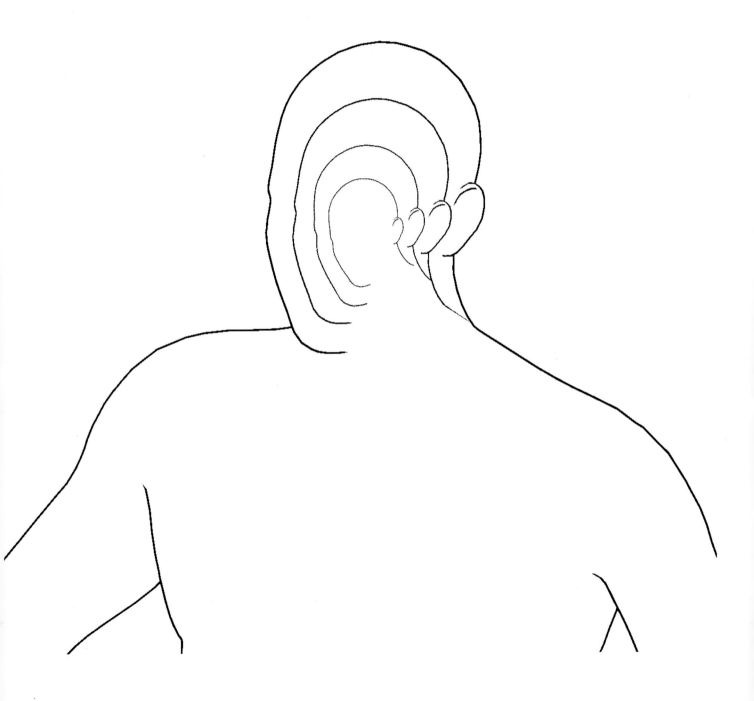

Metaphors
A figure of speech or expression.

51/100

"Less is more" is a metaphor that gained popularity through the works and words of architect Ludwig Mies van der Rohe. He used this metaphor to clarify his design philosophy without using more familiar and forgettable words, like simplicity or minimalism. Examining his architectural and furniture designs reveals his design conceit, prioritizing restraint without compromising beauty.

Metaphor, in design, means clarifying complex or unique problems and solutions; however, interpreting metaphors requires creativity and analysis. Out of context, "less is more" could be interpreted in many different ways. Is less money better than more money? Probably not.

Metaphors construct mental images. They are figures of speech not intended to be used or interpreted literally; when effective, they create an immediate and lasting connection with an audience. You should use metaphors to clarify abstract concepts; however, they should never weaken your story's premise. They should never be the star of your story, just a supporting vehicle.

Metaphors are most effective when they use expressions that are relatable and recognizable. *"Life is a rollercoaster."* Some metaphors are excellent at conjuring imagery in the minds of your audience. *"It's raining cats and dogs."* Metaphors can also arouse emotional and empathetic responses. *"The guilt weighs me down."* This literary device could also translate things that are larger than life. *"All the world's a stage, and all the men and women merely players..."*

Metaphors are excellent tools for comparing one problem with another, and they also act as practical tools during brainstorming and problem-solving exercises. They help frame and re-frame the similarities and differences of stated problems and often redirect the search for solutions that have evaded the creative process.

Metaphors do not have to live in the exclusive domain of words; visual metaphors are equally effective.

The visual metaphor compares things graphically and pictorially through juxtaposition, fusion, and replacement. Juxtaposition—or the least complex of the three—compares two things, placing the design next to what it is being compared to. Fusion combines a design with something that supports its essence, offering a singular visual entity that strengthens its meaning and value. Replacement—the most difficult of the three—visually replaces your design with something else (referred to as a contextual metaphor).

See also:
Analogy (Design by Analogy, DbA) | Hyperbole | Lexicon

Metaphors are most effective when they use expressions that are relatable and recognizable.

"Life is a rollercoaster."

Some metaphors are excellent at conjuring imagery in the minds of your audience.

"It's raining cats and dogs."

Mise en Scène

Putting onto the stage. Setting of the scene. Look of the scene.

52/100

Typically in theater, mise en scène encompasses the arrangement of sets, props, lighting, and composition to communicate nuances that words alone cannot capture. This principle underscores the intentional organization and display of scenic elements that infuse your design and story with context and significance.

Sets include the environment where you will be telling your story or the environment where the design is intended to be used. If your design is meant to be used in a kitchen, speak about the kitchen. If your design is intended to be used in an airport, describe the ideal airport.

Props comprise all peripheral products, prototypes, or exhibits required to use or describe the design's mechanics and aesthetics. If you tell your story in a live environment, what props will help define its purpose? Props could be used to illustrate pure function or metaphorically to depict more complex utility.

Lighting, in mise en scène, while primarily associated with stage lighting, should be considered when presenting a story in a live venue. Determine whether lights should be on, off, or dimmed. Also, consider if any special lighting is recommended or required to use your design effectively.

Costumes, like lighting, sit primarily in the domain of theater and film; however, it is essential to consider any clothing that should be worn while using the design. And if you are telling the story live or virtually, your attire can impact the overall perception of the narrative.

Actors include the individuals designing, using, and supporting the offering. While the design is the focus, including the actors contributing to its success is crucial. Incorporate information about archetypes, personas, or ethnographic research to transform product descriptions into compelling experiences.

Composition considers how each element mentioned above is composed to enhance the storytelling. This involves creating a cohesive and impactful arrangement of elements surrounding your design. These elements add depth to your design narrative.

By incorporating mise en scène into your design narrative, you elevate it into an immersive and multidimensional experience.

See also:
Dramaturgy | Show, Don't Tell | Plot

Mission | Vision | Value Statements

Short stories that explain what is, what will be, and the value you bring.

53/100

When crafting a design narrative, always include the design's purpose, aspirations, and values. They enable your audience to grasp what you do, what you intend to do in the future, and the distinct value(s) you promise. When well-written, each statement will stand on its own; however, they work well together, acting as an indispensable North Star declaration and impactful elevator pitch when time is limited. These statements ignite curiosity, influence action, and encourage confidence.

Begin by answering these four questions.

1. What is the purpose of your design?
2. How do you intend to improve or innovate in the future?
3. What unique value does your design offer and promise?
4. Why did you design this solution, and how are you uniquely qualified to deliver it?

Let's delve a bit deeper:

Mission Statements: These concise, often one- or two-sentence statements encapsulate the purpose and intention of your design or design organization. When formulating a mission statement, always be authentic and direct; remember, a mission statement is what is happening now. Be specific. Whatever you say in a mission statement must be feasible, reasonable, and distinctive.

Vision Statements: Your vision should briefly express your aspirations and the future intentions of your design(s) and design organization. Here, you are painting an alluring picture of what will be instead of what is. Your vision statement should be inspirational, progressive, motivating, and optimistic.

Value Statements: These statements encompass your design and organization's real or perceived value. They include the quantitative and qualitative value your design provides and the core values that define you and your organization, embodying your beliefs, principles, and foundational ideals.

Here is Southwest Airline's well-articulated statement: Connect people to what's important in their lives through friendly, reliable, low-cost air travel. To be the world's most loved, most efficient, and most profitable airline. Southwest will provide a stable work environment with equal opportunity for learning and personal growth.

Crafting compelling mission, vision, and value statements demands precision. To sidestep the trap of verbosity, compile a comprehensive list of action words that encapsulate your organization's essence. Prioritize the top three to five impactful words, and craft your statements. Test with both internal and external audiences to refine and validate your statements.

See also:
Calls to Action | Jobs to Be Done | Lexicon

Compile a comprehensive list of action words that encapsulate your organization's essence.

Music
A metaphor for harmonious storytelling.

54/100

Close your eyes for a moment and envision a formidable, enraged shark. Now, think about a film whose antagonist is a formidable, enraged shark. Like most people, you'll probably be reminded of the film *Jaws*; and then two of the most memorable musical notes composed for a film will likely come to mind. Now, think about how amazing it would be to have an audience recall your stories with equal clarity. Why not borrow from music composition to inspire the composition of your design stories?

In music, the job of a bar or measure is to compartmentalize time to a number of beats. Within a bar or measure, notes sit on one of five horizontal lines called a staff. The placement of a note on the staff indicates its aural quality or instructions to the musician on which notes to play. Within a measure, other notations include how loud, soft, or separated one note should be from the previous or subsequent note. The bounds of a measure are represented by bar lines (vertical lines) indicating where one measure ends and the next begins. These notations produce melodies, harmonies, and rhythms that we recognize as music.

The imaginable combination of notes and beats that can be placed within a measure of music is calculable but vast. However, the complexity and quantity of notes do not reliably determine the success of a musical arrangement. The idyllic composition of notes succeeds when they evoke an emotional response and nourish listeners' memories. In the domain of design stories, the possibilities are equally boundless. Much like a well-composed piece of music, stories live in symbolic measures bound by time and conveyed with an experiential quality that captures the attention of its audience. The finest design stories seamlessly weave together the optimal combination of words, sentences, and paragraphs. Success hinges on the harmonious fusion of these elements, where the conclusion of one word, sentence, or paragraph seamlessly transitions to the next.

Consider iconic films like *ET*, *Indiana Jones*, *Star Wars*, and yes, *Jaws*; each is distinguished by emblematic musical themes that were composed (designed) with remarkable efficiency by John Williams; each composition remains in the viewer's memory long after the film is over. Additional parallels could be drawn from Tchaikovsky's epic *1812 Overture* or Maurice Ravel's repetitive yet intensifying *Bolero*. Even John Cage's unconventional *4'33"*, consisting of nothing but silence, prompts contemplation. Reflect on your design narratives in the context of musical measures, contemplating how words and expressions contribute to the cohesive and harmonious composition of your design stories.

See also:
Gestalt | Rhythm and Silence | Sensemaking

Narrative Design
A text-based description of your design's experience.

55/100

Narrative design offers an efficient means to communicate a design's intent without the resource-intensive process of creating high-fidelity prototypes. Rooted in game design, narrative design articulates the player's engagement with the game's story. This method validates the goals and functionalities of a design in a low-tech manner—exclusively through text. It serves as the vehicle through which a design's experience is conveyed. This type of narrative is often shared with potential users to corroborate overall function and test acceptability. It is also helpful for a design and development team to iterate on a design before it is shared with users or enters the execution phase.

For example, let's take the task of checking into a flight using a mobile phone. After securing a flight reservation, the user expresses interest in receiving a notification for check-in. The process unfolds as follows:

1. The user **opts** for notification via text and **verifies** their mobile number by **selecting** a corresponding radio button.
2. Twenty-four hours before the flight, the user **receives** a text containing a link that **prompts** them to check in for their flight to Los Angeles.
3. Upon **tapping** the link, the airline's application **opens** to the flight details page, encompassing seat assignment, potential delays, and projected weather at the destination.
4. At the bottom of the screen, there is an **option to continue**. Upon **selection**, a new screen will appear with the option to **upgrade** or **proceed** and **obtain** a digital boarding pass.
5. **Opting** for an upgrade, the user is presented with a screen displaying available upgraded seats and associated costs.
6. The user **selects** seat 3a and is **prompted** with a screen confirming payment for the upgrade.
7. **Confirming** the upgrade, a payment screen appears, requesting the user to specify their preferred form of payment, including their credit card on file.
8. **Selecting** the card on file, the screen re-renders with a **confirmation** of payment and updated flight details reflecting the new seat assignment.

Note the bold words above. These are known as speech acts, each signifying the type of interaction or behavior required. Speech acts also prompt the design and development team, informing them of the necessary interactions. A design team could create a consistent list of speech acts across all designs or develop new speech acts for each design. One could see how easy it would be to reduce the complexity of a design in the very early conceptual stage by creating a narrative design.

See also:
Lexicon | Master Planning | Narrative Intelligence

One could see how easy it would be to reduce the complexity of a design in the very early conceptual stage by creating a narrative design.

Narrative Intelligence
The ability to listen, understand, and analyze narratives.

56/100

Narrative intelligence (NI) is analogous to emotional intelligence (EQ). Designers typically have a high emotional intelligence, including being self-aware, motivated, empathetic, with strong social skills, and self-regulating (when necessary). If these traits were not part of who we were, we'd never be able to design for other people, and for those designers with low EQs, their work is likely vainglorious.

Narrative intelligence posits a similar spirit as EQ but for storytelling. The birth of NI was prompted by the broad acknowledgment that storytelling had the distinct ability to galvanize the domains of business, academia, science, engineering, and design. No different than the desire to improve one's emotional quotient, a movement began to explore and improve narrative intelligence to enhance storytelling skills for those whose success depends on persuading or convincing humans to act. Undoubtedly, designers fit squarely into that category.

There are several ways to improve your NI.

1. Cultivate a keen awareness of stories told from a diverse spectrum of individuals. Take cues from mul-

tiple genres. Engage in strategic listening sessions, ensuring you diversify the types of people you listen to. Like EQ, NI is often realized by observing it in others.

2. Practice your storytelling skills at every opportunity, and observe the reactions of your audience. Are they bored and distracted or engaged and interested? Pause and consider how your storytelling tactics resulted in a desired action.

3. Create a storytelling culture within your design group. Spend time telling and politely critiquing your stories before a design is revealed to a client. In the past, I have held monthly storytelling sessions where designers stood up and were encouraged to tell any story they wanted.

Do your best to understand how the stories you hear transform data into wisdom. Always remember that storytelling is a two-way street; engage your audience, and get them involved when possible. Finally, consider the stories that have influenced your actions, learn from them, and use them to optimize your narrative intelligence

See also:
Dramaturgy | Mentalese | Synaptic Pruning

Do your best to understand how the stories you hear transform data into wisdom.

Narrative Transportation

The experience of being fully immersed in a story.

57/100

People who experience deep emotional responses during the telling of a story experience a phenomenon known as "narrative transportation." This occurs when a story is so captivating that it profoundly influences its audience's emotions, attitudes, and actions. In the grip of such a narrative, the real world fades into the background, and individuals willingly suspend their disbelief, setting aside their preconceptions and opinions in favor of complete immersion.

Among all species, humans possess the unique capacity to embrace an alternate reality to serve various purposes: survival, fostering creativity, addressing psychological needs, achieving self-fulfillment, and nurturing faith. When the lights come up after a movie, when the book's last page is turned, or when a story reaches its conclusion, a transported audience may struggle to detach themselves from a narrative. Such a high level of engagement can lead to the narrative being etched into the audience's memory, either temporarily or permanently.

Why do we allow ourselves to be transported? The most obvious reason is that we enjoy it. It provides a sense of escape and pleasure. However, when the content of a story is unpleasant, frightening, or upsetting, transportation teaches us how to adapt to those fears. It might take a bit of encouragement to transport an audience. After all, you are asking them to embrace a world model and a set of beliefs that might be unfamiliar, unpleasant, or unnerving.

Here are three fundamental ways to achieve narrative transportation:

1. Limit the potential for counterarguing by providing just enough facts and information to reduce the likelihood of an audience disagreeing with the narrative's premise. Proper exposition reduces the potential for counterarguing.

2. Enhancing the connection between the audience and the characters plays a crucial role in narrative transportation. Characters featured in commercials, films, or novels must be relatable to their audience to effectively facilitate transportation. When telling a design story, incorporate details about the materials used and how they will make a consumer feel, the intended location of use, and the anticipated user's satisfaction level.

3. Affecting an audience's perceptions with strong and intense imagery, words, and overall depictions related to our senses enlivens a narrative and influences transportation. I recall a 30-second radio commercial that described fresh bread being pulled from an oven, steam wafting from the golden-brown crusty surface, and the sound of the bread being cut made my mouth water. I was quickly transported and drove to the local bakery soon after.

See also:
Affect as Information | Emotion | The Willing Suspension of Disbelief and Poetic Faith

When the lights come up after a movie, the book's last page is turned, or a story reaches its conclusion, a transported audience may struggle to detach themselves from a narrative.

Observing
Watching humans being.

58/100

I take executives and leaders of sovereign governments out of the boardroom and into the real world, where we observe the interactions between people, technology, and designed experiences. I call these events "safaris," and they are very rewarding. Over several hours or days, my clients observe humans being (often my client's customers) in their natural states of work, play, and social dynamics.

In a previous design initiative, my objective was to investigate the frequent misplacement of television remote controllers. Instead of relying solely on quantitative research and surveys to determine the frequency of these misplacements, I chose an immersive, observational approach. I spent a week observing four families in their homes, gaining valuable insights.

It became clear that while the remote control was essential, it lacked subjective value for the families involved. Despite recognizing its importance, the device didn't feel or look valuable, which led to its casual misplacement. To address this, our design solution focused on enhancing the remote control's perceived value. We discovered that other electronic items held a higher symbolic and subjective value. Leveraging this information, my design team prototyped a new form factor

for the remote. Although misplacements still occurred, there was a noticeable decrease in incidents. The face-to-face observation was pivotal in informing the redesign, and we were able to share a story that resonated with our client.

When observing humans, a few tools and methodologies will help. Start by ensuring you have a camera and voice recording device—your smartphone will do. Always seek permission before capturing images or videos. While taking notes, focus on key behaviors and usage patterns. Use shorthand and avoid overwhelming details.

Transform your shorthand notes into a narrative format, adopting a second-person perspective. Craft the story as if the reader is in the main character's shoes, using the pronoun "you" to create a unique and immersive narrative. This writing style, prevalent in immersive role-playing games, self-help books, and marketing materials, establishes a direct connection with the audience. Make note of any changes in affect and assign a score based on intensity, ranging from mild to strong. This approach will enhance your understanding of human behavior and provide excellent material for storytelling.

See also:
Archetypes | Ceremonies and Rituals | Human Technologies

Performance
The telling of a story.

59/100

Is there a difference between performing a story and telling a story? The simple answer is that they are not mutually exclusive. A performance inevitably unfolds whenever an individual steps into the spotlight, addressing a single person or an audience of thousands.

The critical distinction between performance and storytelling is that storytelling fundamentally revolves around the relationship between the storyteller and the audience—an interactive exchange. In this scenario, there's no need to assume a different persona. Stripping away your genuine self from the storytelling diminishes the story's impact and your authenticity. In the context of designers narrating a story, the focus should be on the audience appreciating the design or design methodology without being overshadowed by a flashy performance. I recall one occasion when I thought the audience would enjoy a joke. It failed quickly, and I learned I was not a standup comic. The result was an extended bout with stage fright.

Many designers falter in storytelling because they are preoccupied with performance, acting, and creating a spectacle. On the other hand, I have witnessed designers who deliver monotone and generic stories and lose their audience's attention. While some designers excel at both, many grapple with self-consciousness or stage fright. The principles outlined in this book aim to provide methods for structuring stories, minimizing the need for an extravagant performance.

Here are a few thoughts that reduce the impulse to perform:

- Conduct research to understand why a particular audience might be interested in your design and associated story.
- Maintain interactivity in your story. Monologues transform stories into dull performances. The interactive nature of storytelling boosts energy, influence, and action.
- In storytelling, pauses are essential. Allow yourself moments to breathe and regroup. Acknowledge your humanity to the audience. If you lose your way, admit it, find your place, and continue.
- Pose questions to your audience, preferably ones that require concise answers.
- A potent storytelling method is incorporating personal experiences related to the topic. Share how you were inspired to design the featured elements, the impact it had on you and those around you, or the transformation prompted by the design.
- Conclude with a compelling call to action, cultivating an ongoing dialogue with your audience.

See also:
Calls to Action | Narrative Intelligence | Show, Don't Tell

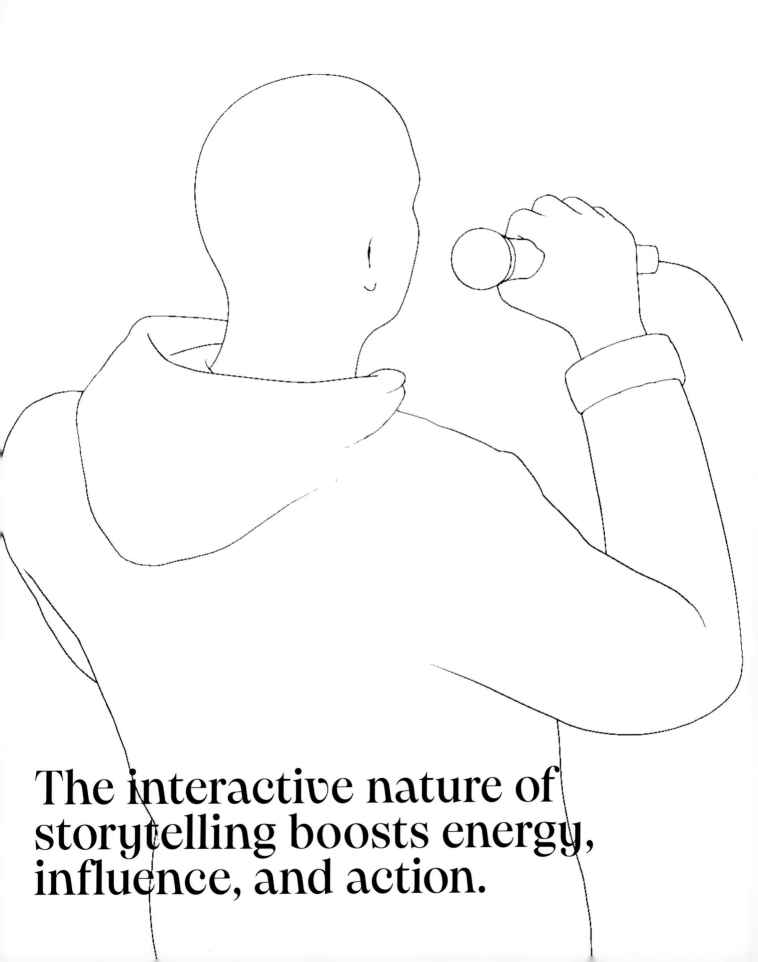

The interactive nature of storytelling boosts energy, influence, and action.

Personas
The fictional representation of real humans.

60/100

Personas are fictional representations of users that expose the essence of humans who will eventually use your design. Personas should never be created from one's imagination; they must be the direct result of observing real people in real situations who express their needs, behaviors, and goals. Personas act as a proxy for eventual users, allowing designers to create with purpose, accuracy, and empathy. A design story without a persona is like a fictional story without antagonists and protagonists.

Let's assume your design story begins by identifying a problem or opportunity that requires a solution. This introduction must be quickly followed by disclosing for whom the problem or opportunity exists—the personas. The personas you cast in your story must be created based on the attributes of real humans. Proper persona research would never send a group of lactose-intolerant humans to an ice cream shop or vegans to a steak restaurant.

There might be occasions where your design story requires more than one persona. For instance, the primary persona—the individual who is the principal user—might be followed by secondary personas that support the principal user physically, technically, or emotionally. Tertiary personas might represent individuals with interest in your design, like stakeholders or collaborators. Once a comprehensive list of personas is created, it is essential to establish their qualities, similarities, and differences.

When telling your design story, you should include an image (photograph) of your persona, immediately making him seem real. Incorporate as much data as possible, including their age, values, likes, and dislikes, as well as what challenges they face that will be satisfied with your design.

Poorly executed personas could lead to unfortunate consequences, including:

- A design story that misaligns with consumer requirements.
- Form and function that are immaterial to real users.
- The loss of credibility when your clients and users do not recognize themselves in your story.
- Stories that include extraneous features and unfamiliar user experiences.

See also:
Archetypes | Character Relatability | Empathy

A design story without a persona is like a fictional story without antagonists and protagonists.

Phenomenology
The exploration of phenomena and human experience.

61/100

Jan Brueghel the Elder and Peter Paul Rubens created a collection of five allegorical paintings depicting smell, sight, touch, hearing, and taste (*Five Senses*, Antwerp, 1617–18). This collection demonstrates how sensory details contribute to the reception of a story. Gazing at this pictorial essay calls on past experiences, enabling the viewer to recollect the senses they experience every day. For instance, the painting in this collection that represents smell portrays Cupid and Venus in a beautiful garden bursting with fragrant plants and flowers. Next to Venus lies a genet, known for its ability to produce an unpleasant musk-like scent, reminding us that not all smells are pleasant.

In philosophy, this phenomenon is known as "qualia"—the direct, subjective experience of a mental state. Rooted in phenomenology, which explores the structures of experience and consciousness, it examines how we perceive and understand the world. Phenomenologists focus on the relationship between how things appear to us and their underlying reality, emphasizing the subjective nature of our interpretations.

A defining feature of phenomenology is intentionality, which has to do with directedness toward something. A person's thought is always about or directed at something specific living within our consciousness. When viewing the Brueghel/Rubens paintings, one's consciousness is directed toward the senses aroused by the images. While this typically references something material, it can also reference something in our imagination or perception—like a unicorn or rainbow.

There is a distinction between illusion and reality—or the way things seem to us and how they truly are. For instance, a rainbow looks real but is an illusion. The moon appears self-lit, but we know its luminance is a factor of the sun's position. The fact that you see the moon means you are conscious, and each conscious state has a qualitative character; each feels like something. Experiences are absorbed subjectively—meaning they exist in the eyes of the human experiencing them. Your stories and designs provoke a level of consciousness. They are a phenomenon and must always possess intentionality directed at something specific.

Early phenomenologists believed the stimuli (living sense-datum) associated with our consciousness are delineated between the mental and physical. The mental phenomena include the potential for imagination, interpretation, and judgment. Physical phenomena are based on the objectivity of space, proximity, density, and other somatic attributes. When I am in Paris, my perception of the Eiffel Tower is shaped by its defining characteristics. The details alone will not explain what it is like to experience the experience within a stream of life. Expressing how something "seems" in the consciousness of the humans who listen to your stories is indispensable.

See also:
Empathy | Dieter Rams' Principles of Design | Rhythm and Silence

There is a distinction between illusion and reality, or the way things seem to us and how they truly are.

Pixar's Story Structure
Eight steps to exceptional storytelling.

62/100

Numerous storytelling structures exist, varying in complexity. While all these methods have their merits, Pixar's renowned "story spine" stands out as a straightforward, effective, and enjoyable approach to crafting a narrative. This structure also assists in writing problem statements that ultimately inform a design and its story.

Despite its simplicity, this storytelling framework has been instrumental in the creation of multiple award-winning works. Whether you're working on a presentation, a one-act play, or an elevator pitch, consider using this method to elevate your storytelling game.

This is Pixar's story spine:

Once upon a time, there was _____.
Simply said, who/what the story is about, where and when it occurs.
Every day, _____.
Portraying the status quo of the world before things change.

One day _____.
Something happened to disrupt the everyday.
Because of that _____.
Use as many because statements as required to explain and resolve the disruption.
Until finally _____.
The resolution.

Complete the story spine template spontaneously and creatively.

- "Once upon a time" sets the stage by introducing the who, what, where, and when.
- "Every day" paints the picture of the ordinary world before everything takes a turn.
- "Until one day" marks the turning point—an unexpected event forces the main character(s) into action.
- "Because of that" highlights how the main character(s) respond to the disruption and embark on a quest for a solution, with potential twists.
- "Until finally" brings us to the story's climax and resolution, where the world undergoes transformation, and a new equilibrium is established.

See also:
Jobs to Be Done | The Hero's Journey

The side effect of this structure is it can assist in writing a problem statement for a design.

Plot
The sequence of events that keeps a story in motion.

63/100

When I think about plot, I think about a train route with a starting point and an ending destination with many planned stops in between, a sequence of events that move passengers and the train to their destination. Plots do the same thing for stories; they are mechanisms that drive a story from exposition to conclusion. The crucial aspect of a plot lies in the sequence of events that form a cohesive narrative, where each event triggers or influences the next. The plot essentially unfolds as the causes and effects drive a story forward.

There is a misconception that the plot is just a story summary. For a summary to morph into a plot, it must contain the following three Cs:

- **Conflict:** Essential to any engaging plot is the presence of conflict—external clashes or internal struggles among characters. Without conflict, a story lacks substance, meaningful themes, or a cause that seeks an effect.
- **Characters:** At the heart of every narrative are its protagonists. Thus, a compelling plot necessitates the introduction of critical individuals who drive the cause, effect, and storyline. A design could be a character if its purpose leads to change.

- **Causation:** The narrative is propelled by the interconnectedness of events, where one occurrence triggers another, setting off a cascade of plot developments that shape the story.

Are plot and story the same thing? Not necessarily. Stories include a structure of events supporting the overall theme. Plots require a rapport between events that influence other events or why events happened in the first place.

It is worth repeating that conflict is an essential element when crafting a plot and refers to divergent forces that fundamentally disagree. These forces could be internal, where a character struggles with personal conflict, or external struggles that manifest in disagreements or conflict with forces beyond their control.

Conflict drives the plot, but there is no cause or effect without characters. Characters convey and propel conflict forward, bringing an emotional and empathetic element to the plot.

Plots clarify the connective tissue that makes a story comprehensible.

See also:
Contrast, Beginning to End | Gestalt | The Hero's Journey

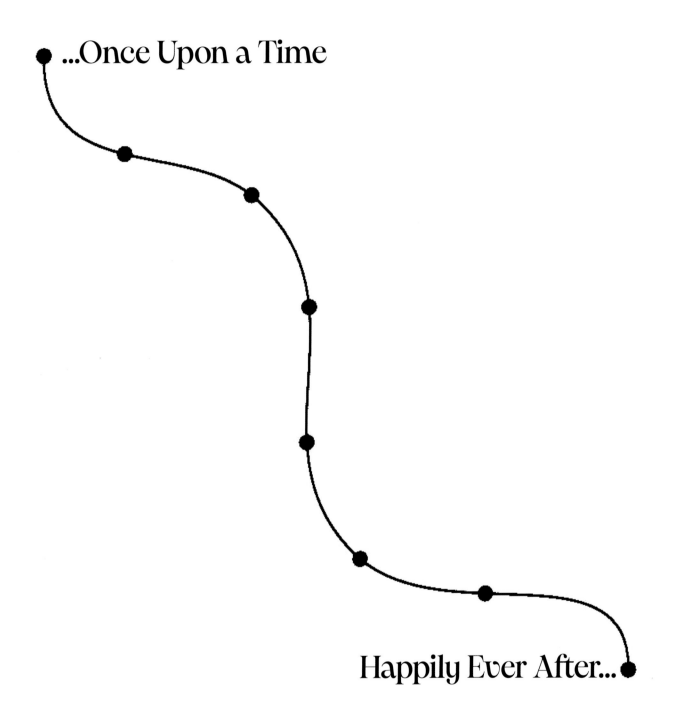

...Once Upon a Time

Happily Ever After...

Presentations
The conveyance of information from one person to another or group.

64/100

By today's standards, presentations often consist of dozens of slides filled with bullet points and generic images, delivering information that, while valuable, fails to leave a lasting impression. Instead of succumbing to this approach, consider viewing PowerPoint or Keynote as a blank canvas awaiting your creative touch. Embrace storytelling techniques like the Hero's Journey to transform your presentation into a compelling narrative.

Here are nine guidelines for crafting effective presentation slides, adapted from the National Library of Medicine:

1. Present a single idea or concept on each slide to maintain clarity and coherence.
2. Keep slides concise, dedicating no more than a minute to each. Let your words complement the visuals.
3. Use clear and informative headings to guide the audience through your content, ensuring they understand the message at a glance.
4. Include only essential points to prevent overwhelming your audience with unnecessary details.
5. Properly acknowledge and attribute sources, including citations for any referenced material.
6. Integrate visuals thoughtfully to enhance understanding, avoiding clutter or purely decorative elements.
7. Limit each slide to between five and seven elements to prevent cognitive overload.
8. Ensure each slide reinforces key takeaways and includes a clear call to action.
9. Continuously refine your slide design through practice and feedback, identifying areas for improvement.

Remember, your presentation should enhance your message, not overshadow it. Practice delivering your narrative without relying solely on slides to ensure your presentation reverberates with your audience.

See also:
Dramaturgy | Gestalt | Performance

Prototyping

The sample or model of something yet-to-be-developed.

65/100

Prototypes serve as tangible representations of designs yet to be realized, a utility that helps assess concepts, functionality, aesthetics, user experience, and the potential for market adoption. While they need not encompass every detail of the eventual offering, prototypes are pivotal in demonstrating a holistic journey while averting the pitfalls of implementing untested concepts.

More importantly, prototypes serve as compelling storytelling props, augmenting narratives by offering real-time demonstrations of the design behind the story. When integrated with storytelling, prototypes foster engaging dialogues, allowing audiences to immerse themselves in the designed experience. They encourage a two-way conversation. While there is a natural inclination for an audience to listen when a story is being told, there is minimal likelihood of active participation unless invited. Prototypes encourage an audience to participate by directly experiencing what it will feel like to interact with a design.

Many years ago, in collaboration with my design partners, we developed a concept for a new retail branch for a multinational bank. The financial services firm that hired us looked at drawings and sketches and read technical specifications but never truly understood the concept because it was an extreme departure from their traditional branch. We decided to build a full-size prototype of the new design in the basement of a New York City retail branch. The entire prototype was white and made of foam core. As we walked the executives through the prototype, we told the story of how customers and colleagues would navigate the environment. The participants could feel the space, touch the walls, and, more importantly, ask questions that helped them clarify the importance of this innovative environment.

This exercise resulted in a group of executives who decided to build several new branches with high levels of conviction. More importantly, we gained positive feedback from tellers, branch managers, and clients, who responded enthusiastically. They began to spread this story of this new environment in their own words.
Not every prototype has to include a full-scale environmental model. Some of my best prototypes were scratched on the back of a napkin and passed around a design studio for feedback iteration and story creation.

See also:
Anthropomorphism | Essence Model | Master Planning

Some of my best prototypes were scratched on the back of a napkin and passed around a design studio for feedback iteration and story creation.

Proximity

The relationship between characters, things, and places.

66/100

The Gestalt principle of proximity posits that objects close to each other are perceived as a cohesive group, illustrating the concept that the whole surpasses the sum of its parts. This principle highlights our tendency to seek patterns that help us comprehend complexity. As you read this passage, consider how proximity organizes letters into words and words into sentences; when letters are isolated from their neighboring counterparts, they lose their significance. Designers harness the power of proximity to effectively communicate information, arranging related, similar, or contrasting elements to create easily digestible compositions.

In storytelling, there exists a parallel concept known as narrative proximity, where creators strategically position story elements to emphasize meaningful connections, differences, or gaps. There are several ways this benefits the storyteller and audience.

1. Imagine a story being told, and your hometown is mentioned during the expositional phase. The immediate effect is reduced proximity between you, the storyteller, and the story.
2. Imagine a design narrative is being told about a new hotel in New York City. While I understand the concept of a hotel as well as NYC, the effective use of narrative proximity would be to indicate the hotel's location as one block west of the Museum of Modern Art in Midtown.

3. Imagine a design narrative with several physical components and an associated service; narrative proximity would require those related elements to be in close proximity.

Narrative proximity serves as a powerful tool to engage audiences by tapping into their familiarity with content and presenting easily recognizable patterns. This concept finds widespread application in journalism, particularly in delivering contextually and geographically relevant content to local readers.

Proximity transcends mere physical or temporal closeness; it extends to cultural, experiential, traditional, and geographical connections. Achieving this requires thorough research into your audience's demographics, cultural nuances, preferences, and aversions to ensure the inclusion of relatable content. Collaborating with designers or partners who understand and embody this proximity can further deepen the connection with your audience.

See also:
Freytag's Pyramid | Maslow's Hierarchy of Needs

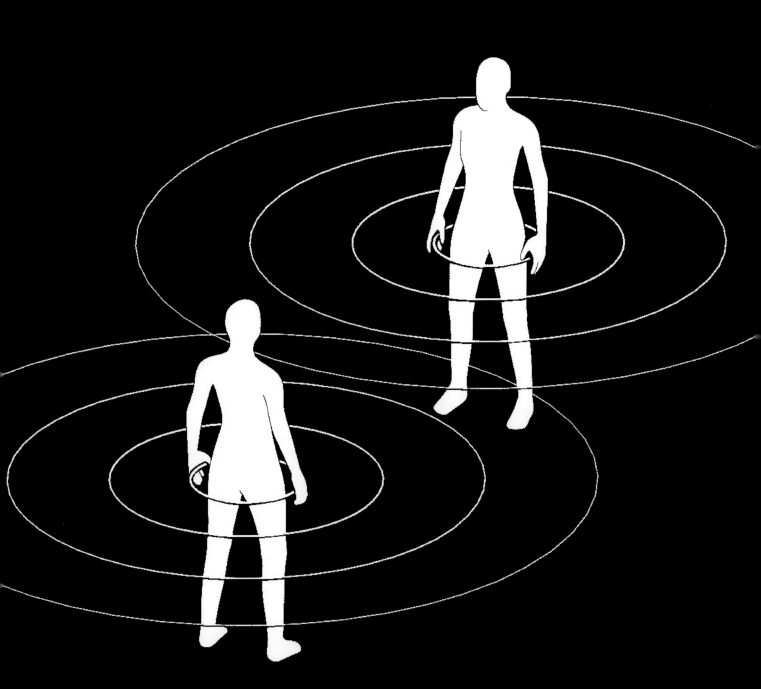

Resource-Based Theory (Marketing)

The story of intangibles that are irreplaceable.

67/100

Storytelling stands as the optimal avenue for illustrating the competitive edge and performance outcomes inherent in your design, your designers, and your organization.

It's widely acknowledged that drawing from marketing principles proves pragmatic, with marketing's resource-based theory serving as the ideal framework to articulate how you can ascend to a position of exclusivity. Central to this theory are four core tenets: value, rarity, difficult to imitate, and lack of substitutability, all of which bolster your competitive advantage and value.

Consider the following questions when crafting your design narrative:

1. Which valuable resources, whether tangible or intangible, enhance the efficiency and effectiveness of your design while also countering threats from competitors?
2. What rare resources do you possess that are held by few others?
3. What difficult-to-imitate assets—such as trademarks, brand reputation, methodologies, patents, or copyrights—does your design organization or your design possess?
4. What "nonsubstitutable" resources exist within your organization, design, designers, or collaborators that are challenging—if not impossible—to replicate?

Given the pivotal role of resources in conferring competitive advantage and value, it's essential to dig deep, define, and categorize everything that demonstrates uniqueness.

When formulating your narrative, consider:

- A comprehensive inventory of your resources (tangible and intangible).
- Your competitive advantage, representing the unique value you offer vis-à-vis your competition.
- Core values or beliefs underpinning your approach.
- Design management practices that embody these values.
- Innovations.
- Your overarching role in serving your clients.
- Any ancillary activities contributing positively to society.

See also:
Dramaturgy | Kano and Storytelling | Theodore Levitt and the Quarter-Inch Hole

Central to this theory are four core tenets: value, rarity, difficult to imitate, and lack of substitutability, all of which bolster your competitive advantage and value.

Rhythm and Silence
The pace and sequencing of a story.

68/100

Rhythm and silence are inextricably linked. One could not exist without the other. The functioning key to music is silence. The key to art is white space. The key to motion is stillness. Ironically, the very thing that shapes how we effectively receive information remains invisible, fueling the rhythm that enables comprehension.

The presence of silent gaps signifies the quiet intervals between each cognitive process (cognitive whitespace). This whitespace serves as a pause amidst the noise, resonating with the Japanese concept of *Ma*. *Ma* embodies an interval or emptiness infused with significance, offering a temporal and spatial pause essential for breathing, learning, feeling, and connecting. Insufficient space across all aspects of existence inhibits growth. *Ma* embodies the transitional space between boundaries where life pauses, granting us a profound insight into the complexities of human existence.

But it takes focus to notice the silence between the beats of life. Watch a group of people clapping to a song's rhythm. There are always a few who are off rhythm. It is not because they don't hear the beat; it is because they pay little attention to the pause, the rest, and the silence that sits between the beats. Rhythm and silence are layers of stimuli that intentionally displace regularity and disrupt symmetry, encouraging humans to move, act, pay attention, and remember.

The patterns that emerge through rhythm guide us daily, helping us envisage our next action, from anticipating the next measure of music to merging a car from one traffic lane to another. Rhythm and silence are the heartbeat of your narrative, guiding your audience through a captivating journey of peaks and valleys that sustain engagement and curiosity.

Tips on incorporating rhythm:

- Vary your sentence length. This is your opportunity to control your story's rhythm.
- Include distinct story arcs where tension is followed by release and divergence is followed by convergence.
- Insert purposeful breaths for the reader or the audience, allowing them to pause, even for a moment.
- Arrange sequences so they flow logically, but don't be afraid to insert an aside that temporarily disrupts and forces a level of syncopation.
- Consider using transitional expressions and words that make it clear you are moving from one section to another.
- Use appositives, or two elements, typically nouns, that sit side by side—one element identifying the other differently. (For example, "My best friend, a doctor, is coming to town.")

Reading your story out loud is always advised to determine if there is enough rhythm.

See also:
Music | Performance | Tone and Tenor

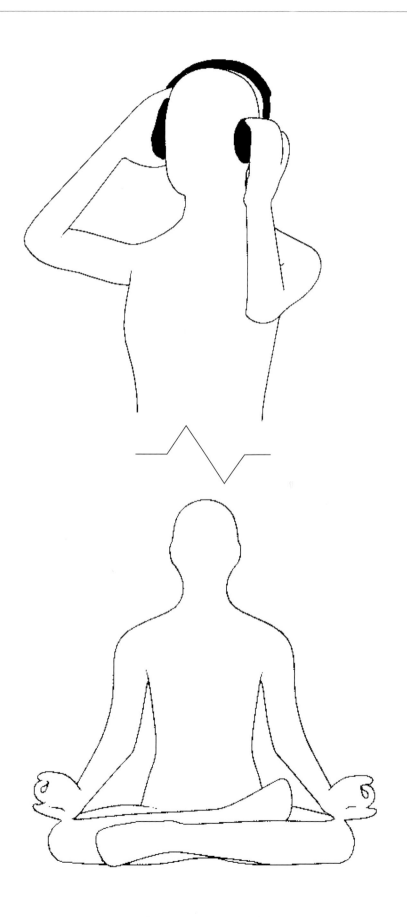

Rule of Three

Items grouped in three are always more memorable.

69/100

Humans are drawn to patterns, enabling us to survive and thrive. They captivate us, help us learn, and remain fixed in our memory. Designers are no strangers to these patterns.

The superpower of patterns is the number three. It is the smallest number required to produce a pattern. The number two is too small, and four teeters on being too big to remember. I could easily remember milk, bread, and eggs, but as soon as my shopping list includes peanut butter, I need to write it down.

The Rule of Three is a storytelling principle that states people better understand concepts, situations, and ideas in groups of three.

When we receive information or become exposed to stimuli, we call upon past experiences that help us determine threats, opportunities, and patterns. The easier it is to decipher a pattern, the quicker we can decide to approach, avoid, or ignore whatever confronts us. And that brings us back to the Rule of Three. Being the smallest number that makes a pattern, it is naturally the simplest pattern to remember.

When using the Rule of Three, always place the most critical point in the third spot. While the first two elements will remain memorable, the last one will dominate. If characters, real or fictional, are part of a story, grouping them in threes will make a big difference. Like in *Star Wars*, we have Luke, Leia, and Han Solo, and in *A Christmas Carol*, there are three ghosts: past, present, and future.

Consider using hendiatris, where three words convey a single idea (for example, "sun, sea, and sand"), and tricolon, which gathers three comparable phrases, words, or sentences characterized by similarity in length, structure, and rhythm (for example, "I came, I saw, I conquered").

See also:
Plot | Rhythm and Silence

The superpower of patterns is the number three.

Sensemaking
Making sense of things.

70/100

Sensemaking clarifies our understanding of the world. Without it, life would be immeasurably challenging.

For designers, sensemaking commences with a deep understanding of the problems or opportunities that call for a thoughtfully designed solution. As designers, we specialize in distilling complexity into clarity, fashioning solutions that reverberate with users because they simply make sense. Design, to an extent, is sensemaking.

Dr. Karl Weick, often considered the creator or "father of sensemaking," likened sensemaking to the utility of mapmaking: "Maps can provide hope, confidence, and the means to move from anxiety to action, from being lost to finding one's way."

Weick offered seven properties of sensemaking:

1. **Grounded in Identity Construction:** Sensemaking begins with the designer's self-awareness and the influences shaping their lives and how they perceive and make sense of the world.
2. **Retrospective:** We make meaning of what is happening in the present by comparing it to events from the past.
3. **Extracted:** People rely on contextual cues to determine the relevance of information and the validity of explanations. These cues serve as anchors, allowing individuals to connect ideas to larger frameworks of understanding. They are building blocks that help people construct a comprehensive interpretation of events.
4. **Plausibility, not accuracy:** Guided by plausibility rather than precision, this approach implies we prioritize perceptions that make sense of an event, regardless of accuracy. Rather than seeking factual correctness, we gravitate towards interpretations that align with our understanding, often leading to compromised decision-making.
5. **Enactive of the environment:** Enactive relates to the actors or people influencing what is being made sense of. These are functions or activities that "sensemakers" cannot control, but they guide and influence our conclusions.
6. **Social:** Sensemaking processes are shaped by the influence of groups and cultures, whether they are physically present or exist in our thoughts or imagination. In interpreting our surroundings, we consider the information others have conveyed and our perceptions of their thoughts or expectations.
7. **Ongoing:** Making sense of things never stops; it is a continuous flow. During that flow, we isolate events, signals, and reflections in order to achieve coherence with what makes sense now and in the future.

Consider these properties as you craft your stories. They will add a unique perspective to how an audience will make sense of your design.

See also:
Deductions | Phenomenology | Stimulus, Organism, Response Theory

Design, to an extent,
is sense-making.

Seven Basic Plots
The seminal list of familiar plots.

71/100

For years, my design narratives were dry and data-driven, often failing to engage. Revisiting my passion for fiction led me to a revelation: Design challenges often align with one of the timeless plots in Christopher Booker's *The Seven Basic Plots: Why We Tell Stories*. These familiar structures resonate universally. Can you think of a design challenge you've faced and link it to one of these archetypal plots?

1. **Overcoming the Monster:** The protagonist confronts and triumphs over a menacing antagonist, whether an individual, a force of nature, or a more significant threat to themselves and the world. Design: A challenge threatens to destabilize an individual, group, organization, or sovereign government, and design is called upon to flex its muscles and defeat the beast.
2. **Rags to Riches:** The protagonist ascends from a humble beginning to achieve success or wealth, faces a setback or loss, and then regains prosperity through resilience and determination. Design: Growth and revenue are shrinking, and a solution must be designed to restore growth and profitability--transforming an organization from rags to riches.
3. **The Quest:** The protagonist embarks on a journey to attain a coveted treasure, reach a distant land, or fulfill a significant goal, navigating through obstacles and challenges along the way. Design: The Quest to discovery, or the need to research or learn something novel that will inform a design. This is the time to leave the studio and observe the real world.
4. **Voyage and Return:** The protagonist ventures into unfamiliar territory, encountering trials, revelations, and danger, before returning home transformed by their experiences and newfound wisdom. Design: Innovation is required, and no stone will be left unturned in pursuit of new value.
5. **Comedy:** The protagonist navigates a series of amusing or perplexing situations, leading to a resolution marked by joy, reconciliation, and a happy and humorous conclusion. Design: Comedic plots in the world of design relate to being creative, pursuing beauty, and although I have always avoided using this word, delight.
6. **Tragedy:** The protagonist's fatal flaw or a significant mistake leads to their downfall, culminating in a catastrophic outcome that brings about their demise.
Design: Telling tragic stories about design failures demonstrates vulnerability. Strength is found in stories of tragedy that teach valuable lessons that will never be repeated.
7. **Rebirth:** The protagonist undergoes a profound inner change or transformation, emerging from adversity or personal struggle as a renewed and improved individual. Design: All stories and all designs result in transformation. These are the best plots to follow as they demonstrate the power of design to renew the status quo.

See also:
Archetypes | Plot | The Hero's Journey

The protagonist undergoes a profound inner change or transformation, emerging from adversity or personal struggle as a renewed and improved individual.

Seven-Point Story Structure

An alternative use for this long-standing narrative structure.

72/100

Although the seven-point story structure can be used to organize just about any story, I have used it in an unorthodox manner: backward. Traditionally, this story structure advocates for sequential events that move the plot forward.

The traditional seven-point structure starts with exposition, where an inciting incident occurs. The structure continues with plot point one, where the inciting incident or challenge is accepted. Plot point one is followed by pinch point one, where a journey (or work) begins. The next element is the story's midpoint, where something happens, making us sit up and pay attention. After the midpoint, we experience another pinch point where the hero, individual, or process faces an obstacle. Another plot point occurs immediately before the story's resolution. A sizeable challenge might sink the enterprise at this point, and the audience may experience profound emotions, empathy, or catharsis. The story ends with a transformative resolution.

I use the seven-point story structure to brainstorm ideas and stories, beginning with the resolution and working toward exposition.

1. Once a design challenge is understood, begin at the end by ideating untamed, moon-shot ideas that present implausible or plausible, but transformative, solutions.
2. Plot point two asks what unexpected, last-minute obstacles might get in the way of success. Explore all potential obstacles, and settle on the most troubling ones.
3. At the second pinch point, doubts might exist about the design team's ability to find a solution to the challenge.
4. We are halfway to the beginning. What major event might take place that accelerates or deviates from success? Can you identify potential and hidden stressors?
5. This story is getting closer to the beginning, and pinch point one reveals how you plan on facing your design challenge, perhaps discussing who will do what to overcome the risks considered in the prior steps.
6. Given how much you've internalized regarding this story, plot point one forces you to examine the story's inciting incident and do some math to determine if it coincides with where you began—at the end, with untamed, moon-shot ideas intended to bring about transformation.
7. You end the exercise with exposition, a fantastic way of determining if what you have at your disposal—the who, why, what, and where—are sufficient to deliver a value-based transformation.

These seven steps can be used forward or backward. At a minimum, the seven-point story structure provides a solid foundation for creating stories that reflect the realities of life.

See also:
Kishōtenketsu | The Fichtean Curve | Three-Act Structure

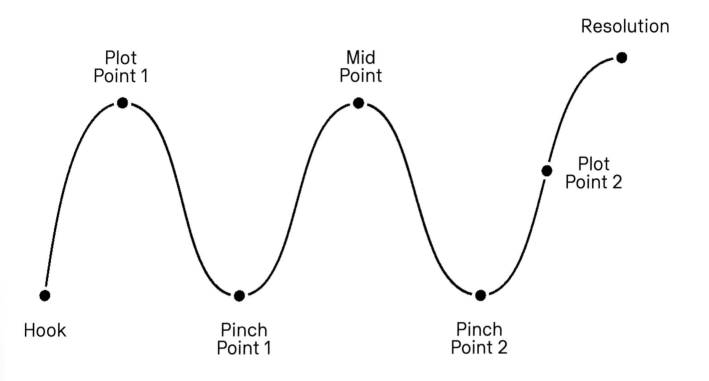

Hook · Plot Point 1 · Pinch Point 1 · Mid Point · Pinch Point 2 · Plot Point 2 · Resolution

I use the seven-point story structure to brainstorm ideas and stories, beginning with the resolution and working toward exposition.

Show, Don't Tell
An immersive storytelling technique.

73/100

Russian playwright Anton Chekhov is credited with coining the phrase "show, don't tell." As the story goes, Chekhov wrote a letter to his brother declaring, "Don't tell me the moon is shining; show me the glint of lights on broken glass." Telling presents concise, factual statements while showing is all about sharing vivid sensory details and descriptions that paint a vibrant picture. Showing immerses your audience in a story. They begin to feel the story instead of just hearing it. Chekhov, in his quote, sparks my imagination. I can visualize the moon in a way that might never have occurred to me. When humans understand what it feels like to use your design, they will more likely covet, buy, or invest in it. For instance, I could describe my first experience driving an expensive sports car in two ways.

It was a red sports car, a convertible. I was warned that it would be loud and that the speed and steering were highly responsive. The leather seats were very soft, and the scent was recognizable as real leather.

Settling into the driver's seat is like slipping into a tailor-made leather glove, every contour perfectly aligned with your body. The vibrant fire-engine red exterior sparkles under the sun's rays, while the engine screams for attention. A gentle tap on the gas pedal will make you feel like you are taking off, not driving.

Show, don't tell is a narrative principle that leads with sensory details, not rote exposition. When well done, your story becomes an immersive experience. Don't force your audience into a state of sensory deprivation; they will always appreciate a narrative that transports them beyond the confines of a descriptive list.

If I am describing, for instance, the OXO Good Grip Peeler, I could say it has a black flexible handle with a sharp silver blade. Alternatively, I could say it's like peeling an apple with a cloud.

How would you change the following three sentences from telling to showing?

1. That was a good chocolate bar.
2. My beach vacation was relaxing.
3. It was nice to spend the weekend with Grandma.

See also:
Meaning versus Value | Phenomenology | The Willing Suspension of Disbelief and Poetic Faith

Don't force your audience into a state of sensory deprivation; they will always appreciate a narrative that transports them beyond the confines of a descriptive list.

Star Trek

The influence of fiction on nonfiction and vice versa.

74/100

In 1967, three astronauts, Roger Chaffee, Gus Grissom, and Ed White, perished in a fire during an exercise for the first Apollo mission. The evening before this tragedy, *Star Trek* aired its nineteenth episode of season one, titled "Tomorrow Is Yesterday." Even in the show's infancy, it offered a glimpse into the future, which stoked the imagination of science fiction fans, many of whom were central members and stakeholders of NASA, the space agency. Despite the Apollo tragedy, the show and its famous Starship Enterprise offered encouragement that the agency's goals would be realized one day, as noted in the *Smithsonian* magazine.

> "*Star Trek* offered hope to a nation and a space program in a moment when both had reason to doubt they would ever reach the moon, never mind the 'new life and new civilizations' promised in the show's opening credits monologue."

Later that year, a dinner was held at the Goddard Space Flight Center in Greenbelt, Maryland. The guest of honor was Leonard Nimoy, who played the beloved *Star Trek* character Spock. The presence of an actor who played this fictional character helped the attendees, who were so closely associated with the Apollo program, heal. That evening, people looked beyond the tragedy. The dinner guests saw Nimoy as more than an actor playing a role; instead, they saw Mr. Spock, a symbol of the future who understood how essential their work was, and, despite the pain they felt, they would carry on fulfilling their mission. Gene Roddenberry wrote the following note to Nimoy:

> "I do not overstate the fact when I tell you that the interest in the show is so intense that it would almost seem they feel we are a dramatization of the future of their space program, and they have completely taken us to heart…they are, in fact, proud of the show as though in some way it represents them."

Storytelling influences humans to explore, discover, and achieve goals previously thought unattainable. I like to think those three brave astronauts who perished in 1967 were inspired by *Star Trek* and believed that one day, humans—perhaps they themselves—would live in space for prolonged periods. *Star Trek* is a textbook example of how fiction and nonfiction influence each other. When crafted with care, stories bring dreams and aspirations to fruition.

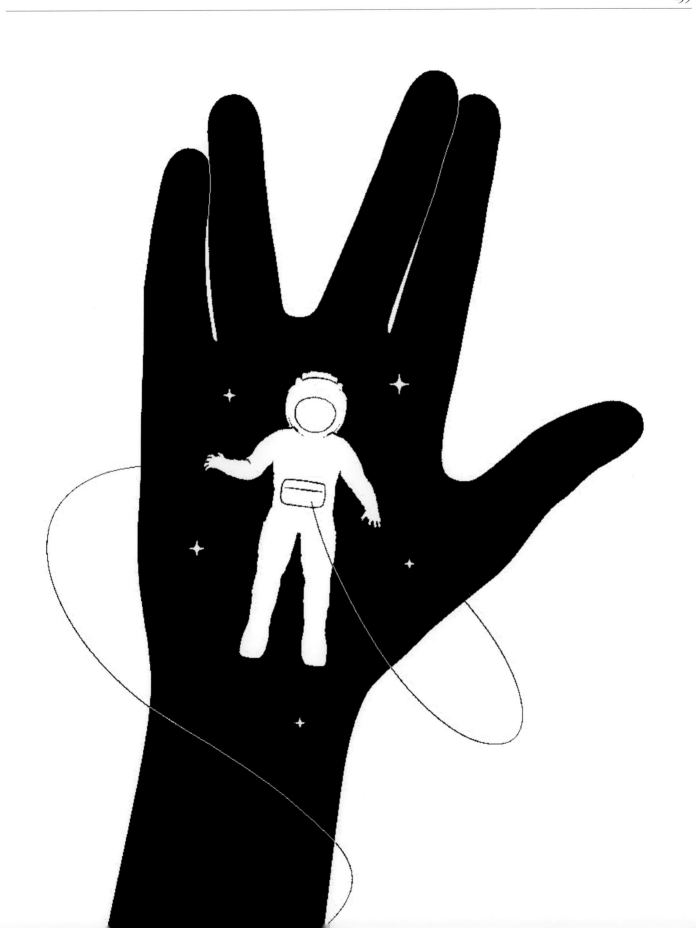

Stickiness
When something becomes contagious, memorable, and hard to forget.

75/100

If something is sticky, it possesses qualities that attract and hold human attention, resulting in higher value, real or perceived.

It is hard to speak about stickiness without mentioning Malcolm Gladwell and Chip and Dan Heath. Gladwell popularized the term in his book, *The Tipping Point*, and the Heath brothers devised six variables that are shared amongst things considered sticky. The acronym of these variables, SUCCESs, is quite sticky itself.

Simplicity
Unexpected
Concreteness
Credibility
Emotion
Story

●**Simplicity:** Your design must eliminate all unnecessary information and represent its essence or core. That said, be sure not to eliminate descriptive elements fundamental to its form and function.
●**Unexpected:** Stickiness requires uncommon and extraordinary ideas that surprise, delight, and amuse an audience. If you've captured an audience's attention, your next task is to maintain that attention by introducing what is unexpected or surprising.

●**Concrete:** All concrete things are easy to understand and lack ambiguity or generalization. One might be absorbed by something unique, but for it to become sticky, it must be understood on a deeper level, including how it affects the senses and emotions.
●**Credible:** The idea is believable and has proof points to substantiate its authenticity and reliability. Credibility without an expert's endorsement must be validated with data, facts, and details.
●**Emotional:** The idea must stir people's emotions, not once, but repeatedly. How do you make humans care about your idea or design? It is your time to touch an affective nerve. This is all about feeling, perhaps viscerally. If you cannot do this on the merits of your idea or design, you might have to resort to presenting analogies.
●**Story:** When things are sticky, stories are told over and over again. But first, your story must include the previous five variables, hopefully generating a quick connection and emotional response. A quick tip is to tell your story, so it is easily repeatable where there are no gaps in understanding. When stories are repeated, designs become trends, habits, movements, and sticky.

See also:
Affect as Information Theory | Hofstede's Cultural Dimensions Theory | Maslow's Hierarchy of Needs

When things are sticky, stories are told over and over again.

Stimulus, Organism, Response Theory (S-O-R)

Stimulus drives organisms (humans) to evaluate and respond.

76/100

The stimulus, organism, response theory (S-O-R) is a concept that hails from behavioral psychology but has deep implications for design and storytelling.

- Stimulus = Story/design
- Organism = Audience/consumers
- Response = Organism's reaction/action to the stimulus

The diversity in responses among organisms raises the question: Why do individuals react differently to the same stimulus? For instance, encountering a snake might prompt one person to move away in fear, while another might pick it up. The different responses stem from past experiences, biases, or deeply rooted fears.

Responses aren't always the result of conscious thought; in their most primal state, stimuli elicit visceral responses that transcend intellect and emotion, residing in the subconscious. Here, the response could be so acute it might cause distress, internally or externally. Internal responses could result in increased heartbeat or sweating, while external responses can range from making a purchase to smiling or laughing. Visceral reactions to stimuli can leave lasting imprints on our emotions, shaping our experiences and responses

for a lifetime. For instance, brief exposure to a scent can evoke tears, bursts of joy, or repulsion.

My father worked for an international airline for decades. When he came home from work, he had the faint odor of jet fuel on his clothes. With every flight I take and sniff the smell of jet fuel, I have a strong emotional response and then think of my father. The trust I had for him, and his exceptional knowledge of aeronautics, provided me with high levels of confidence and a love for air travel.

What does this have to do with design and storytelling. When developing a story or design, there is no way to understand how every organism will respond. The wrong color, expression, texture, or even what you are wearing could set a member of an audience off because of the preconceived stories they have in their minds. Consider any unconscious responses that might transpire and insert additional descriptors that allow your audience to respond consciously, methodically, and logically. If it was made clear that the snake was not venomous and was well-loved pet, the unconscious response might have been different.

See also:
Affect as Information Theory | Emotion | Maslow's Hierarchy of Needs

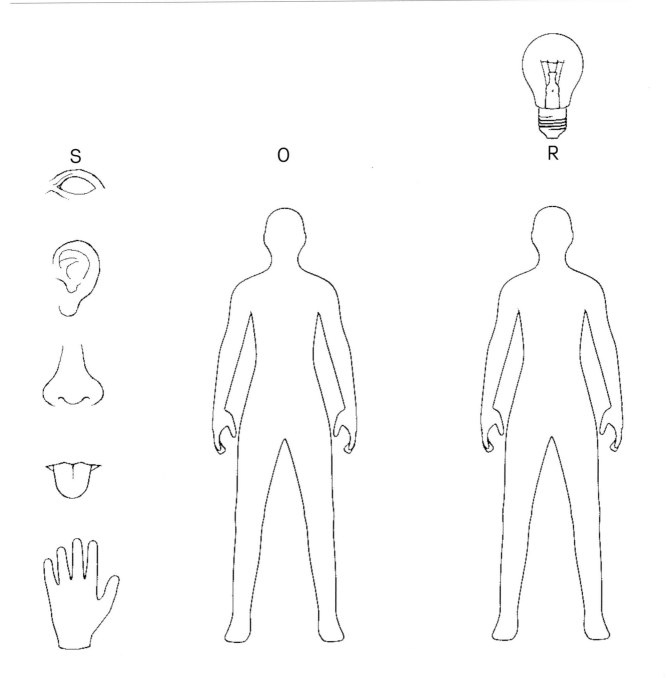

S O R

The diversity in responses among organisms raises the question: Why do individuals react differently to the same stimulus?

Stream of Consciousness

The natural and continuous flow of ideas, thoughts, feelings, and reactions within a narrative.

77/100

Stream of consciousness mirrors the organic, non-linear patterns of human thought. Devoid of grammatical constraints, punctuations, or boundaries, your mind freely navigates its course. It embarks on a journey of free association, influenced by the stimuli in its immediate surroundings. Employed in literature, the stream of consciousness provides a unique window into a character's inner thoughts, akin to eavesdropping.

When viewed through a design lens, we are interested in gaining these rather personal insights from clients, collaborators, and end consumers. A stream of consciousness exercise unveils the thoughts, attitudes, and emotions of a user. This methodology is frequently embraced by User Experience (UX) designers and researchers, particularly during software testing. During these exercises, participants are encouraged to verbally articulate what they are feeling, doing, and thinking.

Designers can leverage the stream of consciousness approach in two ways. First, integrate verbatim first-person transcription of streams of thought directly into your narratives; at a minimum, pull the most relevant elements into your story. This technique lays bare the inner workings of those participating in the study.

Second, incorporate this method into your research practices. The insights gleaned are actionable and valuable inputs for your design practice. This approach is particularly practical when aiming to establish a singular point of view. In cases where multiple perspectives are offered, ensure that each narration, or part thereof, is represented in your story. The stream of consciousness reveals what a person is thinking and, more crucially, sheds light on how they think.

In capturing the stream of consciousness of a participant, I encourage them to use run-on sentences and avoid punctuations unless there is no alternative. If they become stuck or frustrated, they are encouraged to verbalize those feelings.

Engaging in stream of consciousness writing takes the reader on a captivating journey through an individual's mind. It introduces a raw, gritty quality that eludes the constraints of an organized conversation. Reading narration in this form feels like echoing genuine thoughts, departing from the familiar, factual, step-by-step storytelling we've grown accustomed to.

A stream-of-consciousness encourages uninhibited, organic ideas. This can help break creative blocks and reveal hidden perspectives.

See also:
Essence Model | Mentalese

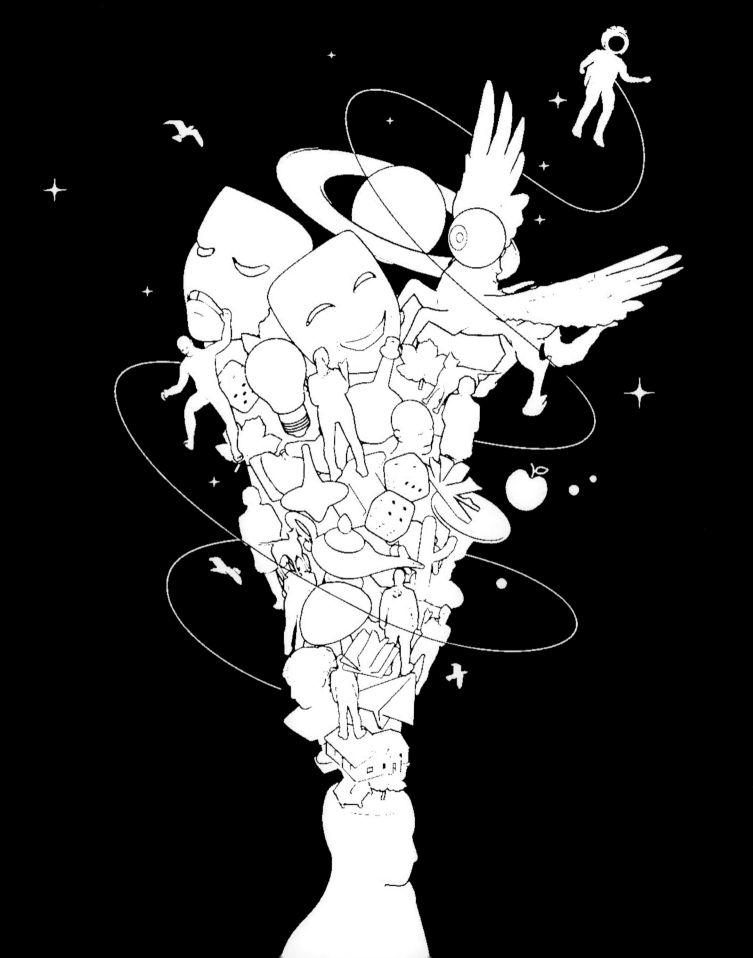

Super Normal
Beauty often exists in what is not present.

78/100

Design is not decoration. Decoration is to embellish, adorn, ornament, or beautify. This is not to suggest that beautification is not one of the many intents of design—it is. However, effective (or beautiful) design could be quite ordinary or, as Naoto Fukasawa and Jasper Morrison call it, Super Normal. Fukasawa and Morrison are world-renowned industrial and product designers. In their book, *Super Normal, Sensations of the Ordinary*, they make clear that design can and should be about absence and that Super Normal is about concealing features and functions with the intent of making them invisible. Super Normal is defined as something that is not present. In the world of the narrative, this is a challenging proposition but one worth exploring.

Fukasawa and Morrison write:

> "Super Normal" is less concerned with designing beauty than seemingly homely but memorable elements of everyday life. Certainly nothing "flash" or "eye-catching"; never contrived, but rather almost "naff" yet somehow appealing. As if, when viewing something with expectations of a new design, our negative first impressions of "nothing much" or "just plain ordinary" shifted to "...but not bad at all." Overcoming an initial emotional denial, our bodily sensors pick up on an appeal we seem to have known all along and engage us in a strangely familiar attraction. Things that possess a quality to shake us back to our senses are "Super Normal."

If the objective or intent of your design and story is to attract attention, the effort ought to be rethought in favor of beneficial or improved function with an emphasis on authenticity that meets a human goal. In its extreme, this philosophy would void any thought of flash or adornment. According to Morrison and Fukasawa, success is not pretending for something to be what it is not. This design philosophy is not void of an aesthetic. The aesthetic is based on simplicity itself. Morrison and Fukasawa ironically propose "leaving out design"; they contemplate that "special is generally less useful than normal." This does not suggest that normal is tedious, dreary, or uninteresting. Morrison and Fukasawa's work is stunning in its simplicity and can act as a muse for future design work and storytelling. The foremost question that must be asked is, "Is an offering well-designed in its most basic purpose or intent?"

What is super normal to you? How might you find the words to describe something that offers little to no obvious descriptive elements but still moves you emotionally?

See also:
Infrathin

If the objective or intent of your design and story is to attract attention, the effort ought to be rethought in favor of beneficial or improved function with an emphasis on authenticity that meets a human goal.

Synaptic Pruning
The human brain has limited capacity.

79/100

Despite the human impulse to tell stories, we often misfire. Our stories fall flat or are misunderstood and sometimes revert to arguments, hostilities, regretful transactions, and dubious relationships. How can something we've been working at for millions of years, something so natural to the human way of being, fail on so many occasions? First, let's look at the brain. It is a very busy organ with billions of cells (neurons) that receive input from external sources that communicate with one another, enabling humans to do the things we do. When synapses are not exercised or become damaged, cells no longer speak to one another efficiently. Subsequently, we lose our ability to be all we can be.

These deficits start at a very young age. For instance, "When a child is born, their brain is not fully formed, and over the first few years, there's a great proliferation of connections between cells," said physiologist Ian Campbell of the University of California, Davis. "Then, throughout adolescence, there is a pruning back of these connections. The brain decides which connections are essential to keep and which can be let go." Neuroscientists call this "synaptic pruning." Essentially, the brain chooses to keep or disregard neural connections based on the frequency of use. In some ways, this is a beneficial human technology that makes the brain more efficient. If we didn't prune now and again, there would be little room for learning new things. There are, however, negatives associated with pruning.

Regrettably, synaptic pruning occurs due to persistent social pressure and institutional "unlearning." Humans are told what to do and how to behave, and deviation from what is considered normal is often punished.

For example, when a child is repeatedly told that her drawings do not look like a person, the synapses that enable drawing are weakened, and the child believes she cannot draw a person. This extends to adults who regularly claim they have no artistic or storytelling skills. A synapse can be strengthened or weakened based on external stimulation or practice. I recall a conversation I had with my daughter's kindergarten teacher. This teacher (synaptic pruner) was concerned that my five-year-old was not coloring in the lines—not following the rules. I knew my daughter understood why the lines existed, but she found it more pleasing to color free-form and explore the potential for blending colors and experimenting with shapes. If I had not abruptly stopped this teacher from pruning my daughter's desire to express herself, she would not have the same appreciation for fine art that she has today.

The point is there will be people in your audience who will not get, interpret, or understand the value of your design story. This is not necessarily because they are disinterested. It could be because the synapses necessary to better understand what sits beyond the status quo have not been exercised in a very long time.

See also:
Affect as Information Theory | Human Technology

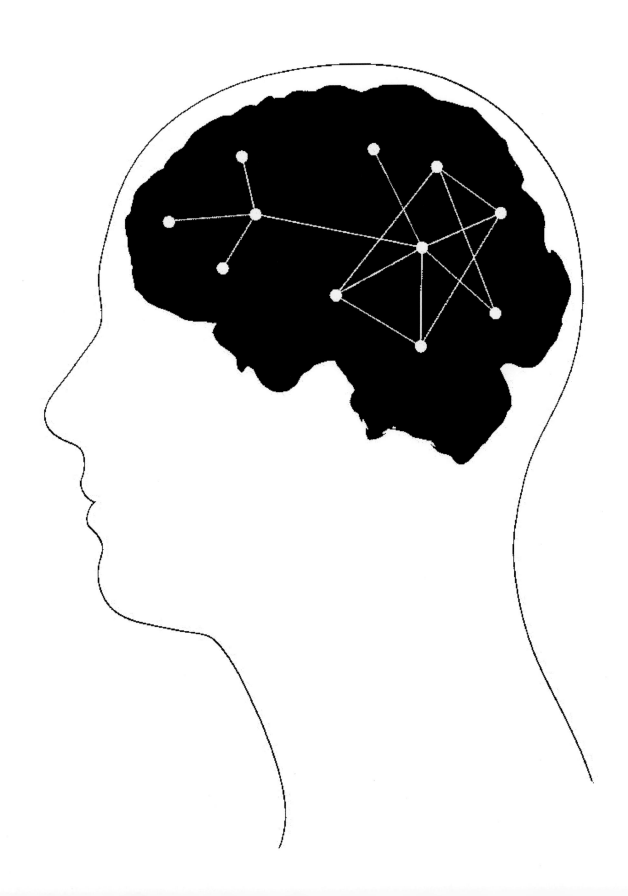

Synecdoche
A figure of speech in which a part is made to represent the whole or vice versa.

80/100

Design narratives that include complex or technical details can be challenging to explain. Storytellers can lean on literary devices like analogs and metaphors in these situations. Despite how rarely the term is used, synecdoche (suh·nek·duh·kee) is an effective way of creating clear connections.

Synecdoche uses a component part of something to express its totality. The reason for using this device is to offer an organic, natural description that leads to poignant, compelling, and suggestive impressions.

There are two primary manifestations of synecdoche: microcosm and macrocosm. In microcosm, a part of something is utilized to signify the whole. An example is "I need a hand"–said when help is required. Saying these four words does not mean you need a physical hand; you just need help. In macrocosm, the entirety of something explains a specific component. For instance, using the phrase *it's a cruel world* describes a subsection of the world, not the entire planet—just a person, group, culture, country, region, or part of a population that is being unpleasant.

Most of us have used synecdoches without even realizing what they are. In design narratives, the most common uses will follow these patterns:

• Describing an object and its material: In this form of synecdoche, the entirety represents the essence of the object, while the part signifies its physical composition. For instance, asking, "Are you paying with plastic?" uses "plastic" to represent a credit card, which transcends its material makeup.
• Depicting a container and its contents: When someone asks, "Can I buy you a glass?" they are not referring to the glass itself but to the beverage it holds, demonstrating a synecdoche where "glass" symbolizes the drink within.
• Describing a category and its constituents: "America took home gold" employs a synecdoche where the broader category of "America" represents American Olympians. This type of synecdoche can also function in reverse, as seen in "the citizens were all put to the sword," where "sword" stands for all the weapons used in the act of killing.

Give it a try. It is challenging but rewarding, and when a synecdoche works, it is often passed along by audience members, becoming a habitual descriptor.

See also:
Analogy (Design by Analogy, DbA) | Hyperbole | Metaphors

"Can I buy you a glass?" they are not referring to the glass itself but to the beverage it holds, demonstrating a synecdoche where "glass" symbolizes the drink within.

The Fichtean Curve
A story structure that focuses on conflict and crisis.

81/100

Have you ever come across a story that propelled you forward like a cannonball, leaving you breathless until its satisfying conclusion? If so, you very likely experienced The Fichtean Curve. Unlike most story structures, Fichtean skips detailed exposition in favor of plummeting an audience directly into a series of challenges, problems, crises, and potential opportunities. And it's not just one challenge; it typically includes a series of complex issues, presented one after another, occurring at the onset of the story.

For designers, Fichtean is perfect for a no-nonsense, quick start to presenting design solutions to wicked problems, where each issue is a symptom of another. The shark-like shape of this story structure is evidence of its objective to clarify the severity of the problems that exist. When this type of story is told, it is persistent and unyielding.

There are three levels to this structure:

1. **Rising Action** requires the revelation of a story's inciting incident; there is no time for extensive exposition. The objective is to create a level of tension by exposing a series of issues that build on one another. Your audience should understand the immensity and complex nature of the inciting incidents. Rising action generally takes up to two-thirds of a story, leaving just enough time for the climax and falling action.

2. **Climax** often manifests as a grand confrontation, pivotal revelation, a profound loss (or gain), and definitely a twist in the plot. It's crucial to note that the climax must be connected to the inciting incident presented during the rising action. The climax does not always result in triumph.

3. **Falling Action** offers your audience some relief. A level of catharsis occurs, potentially revealing how the designed solution will benefit those affected by the crises. Many issues are presented in Fichtean, but not all of them might be rectified or even solvable. This might leave an audience feeling less than satisfied; this is a perfect time to get your audience involved by presenting a call to action.

I have used The Fichtean Curve after an intensive research-and-discovery phase when multiple issues previously undiscovered need to be exposed. It makes significant impact with little need to ease an audience into a story. Although this structure could be used with just about any story, it is best utilized around world issues like global warming, food insecurity, homelessness, toxic politics, or the breakdown of technical infrastructures. Be sure, for maximum effectiveness, to present at least three issues or more during rising action. The intent of this structure is to create and sustain a level of tension until a solution is revealed (if a solution exists).

See also:
Calls to Action | Conflict | The Trigger or Wicked Problem

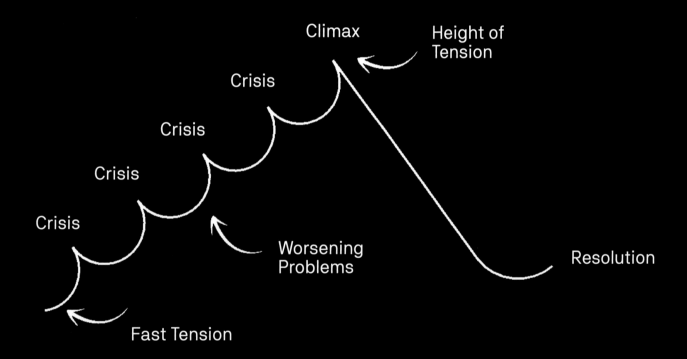

The Five Ps
Product, Price, Promotion, Place, and People.

82/100

The concept of the five Ps originates from marketing, where the art of storytelling reigns supreme. These five pillars serve as guiding principles, ensuring marketers stay anchored to their organization's core components: product, price, promotion, place, and people. This framework is equally applicable to design storytelling, serving as a shopping list of critical storytelling ingredients. By incorporating all five, designers address the critical inquiries of commercial audiences.

Let's delve deeper:

Product refers to your design—a physical, virtual, experiential, or service-oriented offering. Designers will undoubtedly lead with product descriptions, including form, function, benefits, and quality. The key here is to communicate the primary purpose of the design, its value to a defined user, and how it outperforms competitive offerings.

Price is seldom in the domain of design, but I have, during many design briefings, been asked the cost of a redesign, installation, maintenance contract, or percentage of margin. My standard response would be to turn to the salesperson in the room and defer to them; unfortunately, they are not always available. It is advisable to be prepared with an answer, even if it is approximate or analogous to something close to what the audience is familiar with.

Promotion is the telling of your story. However, if a broader promotional scheme is planned or in progress—including advertising, public relations, or digital marketing—it is always sensible to mention these activities. Let your audience know where to look for these promotional spots as a way to continue the storytelling mechanism.

Place, in a design story, includes where the offering could be purchased, serviced, and, more importantly, used. If distribution channels, service offerings, or logistics are associated with your design, this is the time to mention them.

People might be the simplest element of this framework, but they are often left out in favor of a singular focus on the product. It is essential to speak about the individuals who were involved in a design, from the design staff to investors, support colleagues, and, of course, the consumers.

When crafting your design narrative, consider how and where to insert the five Ps. They do not have to be presented in this sequence. It is also unnecessary to go into extreme detail.

See also:
Hofstede's Cultural Dimensions Theory | Human Technologies | Jekyll and Hyde Syndrome

The concept of the five Ps originates from marketing, where the art of storytelling reigns supreme.

The Hero's Journey
The archetypal narrative pattern that traverses time, culture, and religion.

83/100

Some of the most popular stories, in any form, follow the arc of the Hero's Journey. Humans listen, understand, and respond emotionally to this story formula because the trials and tribulations, battles, and victories of the hero are relatable to our own. The Hero's Journey is typified by the adventures of a hero who identifies a problem or challenge that cannot be ignored. To solve that problem, the hero sets off on an adventure/journey to remedy the situation. Throughout the hero's journey, countless experiences force adaptation to known and novel circumstances (no different than everyday life).

The hero's journey begins in a world of status quo, and familiarity—the **common or ordinary world**. We all live in the ordinary world until a calling inspires or persuades us to transform.

The Call is a trigger, prompting the hero to leave the common world and go on a journey to solve a problem or right a wrong. The hero pauses and **weighs the risks** of a journey (the journey's ROI).

A mentor appears when the hero needs support, wisdom, or a tool or weapon to get them through the journey—think Yoda. A mentor could be information that increases the likelihood of success.

The hero **crosses a threshold** from the ordinary world into a special world, where the journey begins. In the film *Jaws*, the sheriff takes one step from the dock to the boat and enters the special world. When work starts, the journey begins.

The hero quickly understands **who will support the journey** and who will thwart the effort. **The cave** is not always a physical location. It is, however, one of the most dangerous spots of the journey—think the villain's chamber, the dragon's lair, the Death Star, or a demanding client.

The hero **confronts their greatest fears**. If they survive the **Ordeal**, they will emerge transformed.

The hero is **rewarded** with a physical item or piece of knowledge or wisdom that will help them endure.

The hero begins a **long journey back** to the ordinary world, but more dangers arise. Climbing the large mountain is difficult, but the descent is just as dangerous.

Resurrection is the **climax** of the journey/story. This is the last test for the hero who is metaphorically reborn.

The hero **returns with an elixir**, a great treasure, or the solution to the problem that prompted the journey.

This structure is scalable. It applies to the trials and tribulations of Herakles or a trip to the market.

See also:

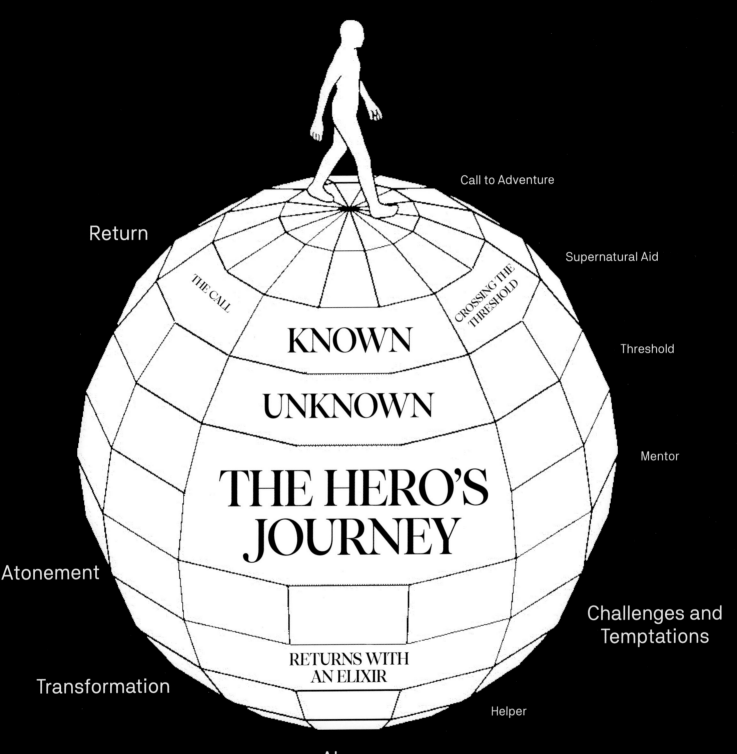

Call to Adventure

Return

Supernatural Aid

THE CALL

CROSSING THE THRESHOLD

Threshold

KNOWN

UNKNOWN

Mentor

THE HERO'S JOURNEY

Atonement

Challenges and Temptations

Transformation

RETURNS WITH AN ELIXIR

Helper

Abyss

Death and Rebirth

The MacGuffin

An object or device that serves as a trigger for the plot but is otherwise useless.

84/100

One of my favorite films is Alfred Hitchcock's *North by Northwest*. An ad executive, played by Cary Grant, is mistaken for someone who is in possession of microfilm containing top secret documents. There are some bad guys in pursuit of the microfilm and the protagonist. While the audience understands the microfilm exists and that it is essential to the plot, the content of the microfilm is never revealed. In reality, Hitchcock never meant for anyone to know the details of its content. He used the microfilm as a MacGuffin, a device that moves a plot along but has little significance otherwise.

All we learn about the microfilm is that it exists. What kind of secrets are on it? Why was it so important that people were willing to kill to get it? All of those details are inconsequential to the story. This plot device merely exists to set the events in motion. We aren't meant to care about the microfilm; it's a red herring. The MacGuffin boils down to absolutely nothing at all, and, ironically, that's what makes it useful.

When and if your design story requires a bit of a push to move things along, consider using or inventing a MacGuffin. While it is unlikely that you have secret microfilm, there are real MacGuffins, and they live in a world of intangibles or assets that are non-monetary and typically without physical substance. Examples of intangibles include licenses, trademarks, patents, brands, proprietary methodologies, and anything else that cannot be touched and maintain difficult-to-assign value. A person or goal can be a MacGuffin as well. Take a moment and consider the intangibles that move your design work along but are seldom mentioned in the stories you tell. Including a MacGuffin could, and should, be used as a catalyst that adds action and momentum to your story.

For instance, I've previously highlighted a patent our team was granted, stemming from work completed years ago. Alongside, I've woven in research methodologies and workshop exercises that unearthed valuable insights, enriching the narrative although not directly tied to the design itself. The aim was to underscore the depth of our research, informing our design decisions profoundly.

Moreover, I've recounted the indispensable role of a team member who wasn't physically present, yet played a pivotal part in the project's success. Simply mentioning their name and a defining trait piqued the audience's curiosity, serving as an excellent narrative device akin to a MacGuffin. This approach, devoid of specific details, subtly underscores the presence of intangible elements driving the narrative forward without needing explicit portrayal.

See also:
Character Relatability | Plot | The Trigger or Wicked Problem

The MacGuffin boils down to absolutely nothing at all, and, ironically, that's what makes it useful.

The Paradox of Suspense
When a suspenseful story remains compelling despite its familiarity.

85/100

I've watched the film *Jaws* numerous times; it's one of my favorites. I'm well-acquainted with its plot, dramatic arcs, jump scares, and the ending. Yet, every time I rewatch the film, I find myself entangled in a state of suspense. Welcome to the paradox of suspense.

Suspense is a complex cocktail of fear, hope, and uncertainty. Emotions such as fear and hope, known as "prospect emotions," depend on how desirable and likely we perceive a future outcome to be. If I believe an undesirable outcome is highly likely, my fear increases. On the other hand, hope rises when an outcome appears both desirable and achievable.

Four theories clarify this paradox, all relevant for storytellers aiming to infuse suspense or maintain an audience's interest beyond its initial telling.

1. **Entertained Uncertainty**: Noël Carroll suggested suspense doesn't require true uncertainty; imagining alternate endings, even when knowing the outcome, can still create suspense. For instance, knowing a tragic event is coming doesn't stop us from hoping for a different end.

2. **Desire-Frustration Theory of Suspense:** Aaron Smuts argued that suspense arises from the frustration of wanting to change an inevitable outcome, not from uncertainty. We may feel powerless and frustrated, not suspenseful, as we watch events we can't alter.

3. **Emotional Misidentification:** Robert Yanal claimed that repeated viewings create anticipation, not suspense, which depends on uncertainty. In *Rear Window*, Jeff's helplessness (being bound to a wheelchair) heightens shared frustration, showing that suspense might be unique to a first viewing.

4. **Moment-by-Moment Forgetting Theory:** Richard Gerrig contended that suspense does require uncertainty. Revisiting a story can reveal new details or interpretations, allowing us to feel suspense through forgotten or reinterpreted elements.

See also:
Affect as Information Theory | Empathy | Narrative Transportation

The paradox of suspense is a complex cocktail of fear, hope, and uncertainty.

The Peak-End Rule

Our memory is affected around the most intense moments and at the end of an experience.

86/100

The peak-end rule, conceived by Nobel Prize–winning psychologist Daniel Kahneman, provides insights into the cognitive biases shaping our recollection of past experiences. Kahneman explains that our memories are often incomplete and influenced by the emotions we felt during those experiences. This explains why our memories can be somewhat irrational since we typically recall highlights and not details or the length of the experience.

Kahneman describes two types of "selves." One is the experiencing self, which is our instant-to-instant awareness or our state of being present. This "self" thinks intuitively, quickly, and unconsciously. In this state, humans seldom remember events past a few seconds. However, the narrating self stores, collates, and builds narratives placed in our database (brain) as a memory. The narrating self edits, interprets, and, in many cases, supplements the experience, quickly becoming the stories we tell.

Consider this: As you tell your stories, your audience is going through this process; eliminating bits of your story that are irrelevant or perhaps uninteresting. They will, however, recall an impactful ending as well as the peaks in your story.

Our brain has a finite capacity to remember every experience we encounter, a mechanism crucial for our survival. It selectively retains memories that contribute to our well-being, discarding those that are irrelevant. Consequently, our recollections gravitate toward the most pleasurable and painful moments, aiding us in avoiding threats and approaching enjoyable experiences.

Whether in design briefs, client meetings, or critiques, it is crucial to strategically incorporate memorable peaks and, at a minimum, ensure a positive ending. This principle holds true even in challenging situations, where concluding on a positive or encouraging note can significantly influence perceptions and outcomes.

See also:
Emotion | Exposition | Phenomenology

As you tell your story, your audience is eliminating parts that are irrelevant or perhaps uninteresting.

The Senses
How humans interact and perceive the world around us.

87/100

I recently had an interesting experience at a car dealership. As I explored a car, a salesperson with a unique approach caught my attention. After giving me a thorough tour of the automobile, he ended with an unexpected demonstration. He opened and closed the driver's side door with a deliberate slam, then looked at me and asked, "Did you hear that?" Perplexed, I nodded, and he repeated the action, emphasizing the sound. The salesperson explained the significance of the carefully crafted sound of the door closing, a detail often overlooked by buyers. While I didn't purchase the car, what lingered in my memory was that distinctive, satisfying thump.

This encounter made me reflect on Edgar Dale's Cone of Experience, which highlights the varying degrees of retention based on how information is presented. We remember 10 percent of what we read, 20 percent of what we hear, 30 percent of what we see, 50 percent of what we see and hear, 70 percent of what we discuss with others, 80 percent of what we experience, and 95 percent of what we teach others. What would happen if we involved all of our five senses as well?

Every design has the potential to engage our senses. Incorporating descriptions of how your design impacts human senses, directly or indirectly, breathes life into your narrative. This approach is compelling because our senses are fundamental to perceiving the world, navigating hazards, and seeking enjoyment.

Sight is the simplest way to describe a design. It has to look like something, but can you stretch the description to something less literal that will strike an emotional yet familiar chord? Benjamin Moore has multiple paint colors in the red family, but they use descriptions like Hot Lips and Royal Flush.

Taste is challenging to embed in a narrative, but the effect is outstanding when it works. You could generalize by saying the way the design performs is sweet, or if it pulls on the side of vibrant, it could even be spicy.

Touch is a sense I often use, including the process, service, or finish being as smooth as silk or a color choice as being hot or cool.

Smell is a sense that stays resident in our memories for a very long time (for better or worse). If you can connect a scent and a design, it will yield a visceral response. I recall describing walking into the famous Parisian department store Galeries Lafayette, like walking through a field of flowers or designing a retail bank branch, hoping the environment smelled like money.

Sound is one sense that could be used comprehensively, such as the car door sounding like the thud of a muffled bass drum or referring to a pattern that is noisy but effective. And, of course, I've been known to say, "This design is like music to my ears." Or, "The silence of this audience is deafening."

See also:
Analogy (Design by Analogy, DbA) | Metaphor | Stimulus, Organism, Response Theory

Incorporating descriptions of how your design impacts human senses, directly or indirectly, breathes life into your narrative.

The Trigger or Wicked Problem

The reasons we tell stories and design things—the why behind the what.

88/100

While some problems are straightforward, only requiring critical and creative thinking, others are more formidable and deemed "wicked." By revealing a wicked problem in your narrative, you share the criticality of a design exercise.

In mythology, a daunting predicament (wicked problem) can equate to a life-or-death struggle for a hero. In the real world, addressing wicked problems becomes imperative due to their potential to trigger severe fiscal, social, and brand crises if unresolved.

In 1973, Horst Rittel introduced ten attributes of wicked problems, primarily around complex social issues.

1. Wicked problems have no definitive formulation. The problem of poverty in Texas is grossly similar but discretely different from poverty in Nairobi, so no practical characteristics describe "poverty."
2. It's hard to measure or claim success with wicked problems because they bleed into one another, unlike the boundaries of traditional design problems that can be articulated or defined.
3. Solutions to wicked problems can be only good or bad, not true or false. There is no idealized end state to arrive at, and so approaches to wicked problems should be tractable ways to improve a situation rather than solve it.
4. There is no template to follow when tackling a wicked problem, although history may provide a guide. Teams that approach wicked problems must make things up as they go.
5. There is always more than one explanation for a wicked problem, with the appropriateness of the explanation depending on the individual perspective of the designer.
6. Every wicked problem is a symptom of another problem. For example, the interconnected quality of socioeconomic political systems illustrates how a change in education will cause new behavior in nutrition.
7. No mitigation strategy for a wicked problem has a definitive scientific test because humans invented wicked problems, and science exists to understand natural phenomena.
8. Offering a "solution" to a wicked problem frequently is a "one shot" design effort because intervention changes the design space enough to minimize the ability for trial and error.
9. Every wicked problem is unique.
10. Designers attempting to address a wicked problem must be fully responsible for their actions.

Identifying a wicked problem is not merely about comprehending the potential returns of one's efforts; it's about grasping the fundamental reason for undertaking the design endeavor.

See also:
Dramaturgy | Phenomenology | Stimulus, Organism, Response Theory

While some problems are straightforward, only requiring critical and creative thinking, others are more formidable and deemed "wicked."

The Wall

The imaginary wall that sits between the teller of a story and their audience.

89/100

In fiction, the fourth wall is an imaginary barrier separating characters and actors from their audience. For example, during a theatrical performance, an actor may momentarily break character to address the audience directly, causing the illusionary fourth wall to collapse. Once the direct interaction with the audience concludes, the actors return to onstage performance, reinstating the fourth wall.

Breaking the fourth wall disrupts the narrative flow to convey a specific (or special) message. Whether interrupting the story with a question, stumbling over words, offering apologies, or spontaneously sharing a personal detail, each instance shatters the illusion of seamless storytelling or the continuity of a theatrical performance.

Breaking the fourth wall offers both advantages and disadvantages in storytelling. It re-captures the audience, reeling them back in if their attention falters.

I've broken the fourth wall to emphasize crucial points during design briefings. However, such instances demand careful consideration to avoid disrupting the story's momentum. If you do this, you might have to remind your audience where you left off unless the break is brief.

In one memorable instance, I recognized the skepticism of my client's chief financial officer. I paused and addressed him directly, reassuring him the return on investment would exceed his expectations. He was clearly out of his comfort zone during the design brief, so I broke the wall and engaged with him directly.

Involving an audience by inviting their thoughts or questions breaks the fourth wall.

During presentations, I often defer to a team member, introducing a rhythm to the narrative while giving myself a moment to regroup.

If you choose to break the fourth wall, do your best to make it seem natural. When executed clumsily, it may come across as disorganized. Above all, breaking the fourth wall should enhance, not overshadow, the narrative. When employing this technique, it's crucial to guide the reader back to the main story, ensuring continuity.

See also:
Dramaturgy | Performance | Show, Don't Tell

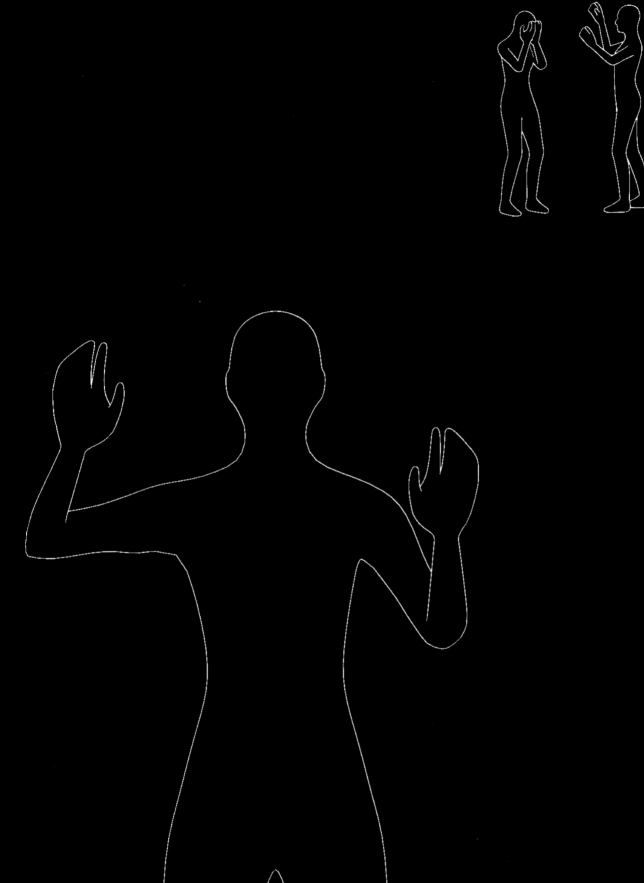

The Willing Suspension of Disbelief and Poetic Faith

Suspending one's capacity for critical and logical thinking to temporarily believe in something that appears too extraordinary to be real.

90/100

The concept of "suspension of disbelief" originated with Samuel Taylor Coleridge in 1817. His premise was that a writer could infuse "human interest and a semblance of truth into a fantastic tale," enabling the reader to set aside judgment regarding the narrative's implausibility. In collaboration with William Wordsworth, Coleridge embarked on an experiment to fashion stories with "supernatural qualities" that could convey a "semblance of truth." Coleridge referred to this idea as "poetic faith," which could only occur when the audience suspended their disbelief.

Coleridge underscored that suspending disbelief is a self-imposed, conscious decision. His thesis primarily pertained to literature and poetry, but "poetic faith" applies to all forms of storytelling, including the landscape of contemporary marketing and design. In a world where individuals confront a ceaseless barrage of meticulously crafted marketing messages every day and every minute, the immediate response often tends to be detachment. In such a scenario, the willingness to suspend one's disbelief may seem beyond reach.

However, when a message captures our attention and prompts a momentary consideration, regardless of its feasibility, we may immerse ourselves in an alternate reality or momentarily disbelieve what we consider true to fulfill our needs.

The following principles assist in fostering the suspension of disbelief and securing poetic faith:

- **Grounding the Extraordinary in Fact:** To encourage an audience's willingness to believe, it is crucial to provide a foundation of facts, even if these facts are artfully fabricated. Whether a story

See also:
Archetypes | Narrative Transportation | World-Building

When a message captures our attention and prompts a momentary consideration, regardless of its feasibility, we may immerse ourselves in an alternate reality or momentarily disbelieve what we consider true to fulfill our needs.

resides in reality or fantasy, a symbiotic relationship between these facts and the narrative's plot is vital. For instance, without explaining Superman's extraordinary powers, the audience would struggle to suspend their disbelief when he takes his first flight.

•**Humanizing Characters:** Characters, whether sentient or not, must exhibit relatable human traits, often drawn from archetypes. These shared characteristics establish a profound connection with the audience, even within the most fantastical stories. Take, for example, Thor in the Marvel Cinematic Universe. Despite his physically imposing presence and unwavering commitment to good, he is portrayed with familiar and vulnerable human qualities, such as jealousy and depression, as seen when he gains substantial weight in *Avengers: Endgame* and appears jealous of his mortal girlfriend, Jane.

•**Consistency in World-building:** The storyteller must meticulously craft and adhere to a defined worldview and set of rules from the story's inception. Deviating from these rules can disrupt the audience's engagement and belief in the narrative. These rules can be extraordinary but must be constructed to render the story implausible but not impossible. The world enveloping the story should, in some manner, appear within the realm of possibility, and the boundaries of what is permitted and acceptable should be clearly established.

Theodore Levitt and the Quarter-Inch Hole

The quarter-inch hole is one of the greatest yet simplest marketing theories.

91/100

The philosophy of Theodore Levitt, encapsulated in his famous statement, "People don't want a quarter-inch drill, they want a quarter-inch hole," has been a wellspring of inspiration for me. Levitt's wisdom underscores the fundamental principle that organizations must understand and fulfill the desires and needs of their customers just as much as, if not more than, the efficient production of goods and services.

Envision a design narrative stripped of technology, form, and function. It would simply include the essence of its outcome, devoid of the details that made it what it is. This notion offers a lens to unveil the spirit and purpose behind a design and its story, transcending its physical or digital manifestation and focusing on why it was undertaken in the first place.

Suppose I was designing a retail store that sold audio equipment. In that case, I might feel compelled to tell a story about where the components sat within the environment, how shoppers would navigate the aisles, and the placement of marketing material. Alternatively, what would happen if I simply told the story of what it would be like to sit back in the most comfortable chair after a hard day at work and listen to your favorite music. Or, if I were designing a self-service device that sold train tickets, I would tell a story about how, after a long day in the office, a commuter arrived home quickly and efficiently to enjoy a family dinner and a child's soccer game.

Levitt argued that businesses often prioritize short-term wins over sustainable growth, a phenomenon he called "marketing myopia." This occurs when companies focus on immediate needs, rather than on customers' long-term desires. For example, the railroad industry saw itself as a railroad provider rather than a transportation provider, missing broader growth opportunities. Similarly, when television emerged, film industry leaders saw themselves as selling film instead of entertainment, ignoring the consumer's true desire: to be entertained.

Craft a narrative solely focused on the human experience, devoid of any design specifications such as objects, screens, processes, or journey maps.

Thesis + Antithesis = Synthesis

A point, followed by an alternative point, followed by a solution.

92/100

While telling a design story, I'm often asked how the design was conceived. Rather than providing a direct answer, I regularly describe this simple but effective method for vetting ideas: thesis, antithesis, and synthesis.

- The thesis is an initial proposition.

- The antithesis negates the thesis and reacts to the proposition.

- The synthesis solves the conflict between the thesis and antithesis by reconciling their common truths and forming a new proposition.

For example:

- Thesis: The new hotel room should include a small sofa and chair.

- Antithesis: The budget will not allow for the furniture, and guests spend little time in their rooms.

- Synthesis: Design a lounge space in the lobby with private and semi-private areas for work and socialization.

With its roots in philosophy, this model offers a simple way to advance ideas and structure answers to questions related to how a design is conceived. An idea or concept is presented, highlighting its advantages and limitations. Through analysis and innovative thinking, designers tackle the obstacles, ultimately arriving at a novel solution.

The most challenging part of this process is the negation or contradiction of the initial thesis, especially for those designs that require a significant amount of time and effort to conceive. This proposition demonstrates that we can navigate challenges through careful analysis and innovation, leading to a resolution that propels us forward.

In practice, there has to be a willingness to dispose of ideas that are not meaningful or do not solve a problem for the defined user or user group.

If you choose to use this scheme, try presenting it this way. The first designer introduces the main thesis; the second designer presents the antithesis; and finally, the third designer—typically the most senior designer—presents the synthesis, showcasing teamwork and thoughtfulness.

See also:
Essence Model | Kill Your Darlings | Gestalt

Through analysis
and innovative
thinking, designers
tackle the obstacles,
ultimately arriving at
a novel solution.

Three-Act Structure
The simplest structure of a story.

93/100

Of all the story structures to choose from, the simplest and perhaps oldest is the three-act structure. Tracing back to Aristotle's *Poetics*, this structure focuses on three story beats or shifts in the way the narrative plays out. According to Aristotle, stories are a chain of cause-and-effect actions, each inspiring the next. Story beats are moments/events that move a story forward, frequently referred to as story shifts.

Each act owns at least one plot point. Together, they make a complete story.

Act one begins with exposition, establishing the story's worldview. The two most essential items that need to occur in act one are describing the status quo before it changes and the inciting incident or catalyst that moves the story along. In most cases, the inciting incident creates an imbalance in the ordinary world.

Example: My client expressed concern that his company was experiencing diminishing conver-

sion rates on its e-commerce site. Examining the status quo confirmed the site had not changed in three years while the competition repeatedly updated their environment. If a redesign did not improve the conversion rates, they would be out of business in six months.

Act two refers to the rising action that devolves into crisis, difficulty, or challenges. A journey (work) begins in an attempt to remediate the challenge or inciting incident. The protagonists (clients) have committed to changing the status quo and will face tasks, tests, and trials, some of which might seem unsolvable and risky.

Example: The client decided they would fund a new e-commerce site; however, some members of the in-house marketing team were disinterested in promoting the transformation, and the expense of the redesign was higher than the client could afford. After an extensive ROI discovery phase, it was proven that the proposed design would exceed

See also:
Calls to Action | Freytag's Pyramid | The Hero's Journey

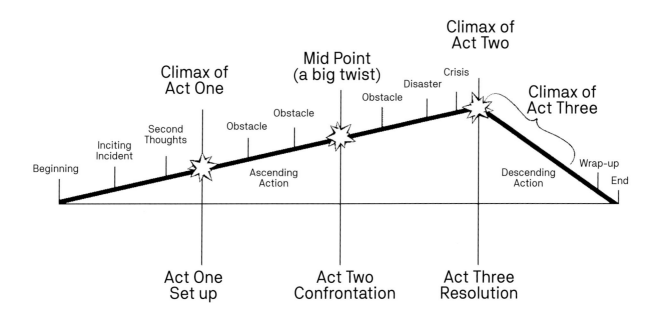

financial expectations, and the design team was given the go-ahead.

Act three typically includes a final dramatic conflict, confrontation, or clash that raises the level of drama and uncertainty to another level. Things unwind at their peak of dramatic tension, and a new status quo or transformation is revealed.

Example: Just prior to the release of the new website, our client's most significant competitor published a new site that was met with high demand. With few other choices, we released the new e-commerce site. The first two days saw little to no traffic, but on the third day, we saw a considerable uptick in conversion rates that exceeded our expectations. Three months later, our client purchased the competitors business.

The story beats in this three-act structure should be clear.

•Act One: The client recognizes their receding role and complacency in the marketplace.
•Act Two: Despite recognizing that survival depends on a redesign, team members are resistant.
•Act Three: Success is not enjoyed immediately, but with patience and confidence, the client succeeds.

The underlined words above are the "story beats." They ensure your story is well-organized, void of complexity, and actionable.

Tone and Tenor
Describing the overall attitude, mood, and depth of a story.

94/100

Every human interaction carries a tune and meaning. Both are essential elements of human expression, often referred to as tone and tenor.

Tone, the melody of communication, paints the emotional landscape behind each word spoken or written. Like a painter's brushstrokes, it shapes the atmosphere and feeling that envelops our expressions. From the biting sarcasm that cuts through the air to the joyful cadence that lifts spirits, tone guides our interpretation of the world around us. In literature, authors masterfully wield tone to evoke a symphony of emotions in their readers, crafting narratives that vibrate long after the story concludes.

Yet beneath the melody lies the substance of our expressions—the tenor. Like the steady beat of a drum, tenor anchors our words in deeper meaning and intention. It is the silent force that guides our understanding beyond the surface, revealing the true essence of our communication. In rhetoric, the tenor of a message can sway hearts and minds, shaping perceptions and beliefs.

While tone and tenor work in harmony, they each play a distinct role in orchestrating human expression. Tone paints the emotional canvas, while tenor lays the foundation of the meaning beneath. Though tone may vary with emotion, tenor remains a constant, guiding light.

Can you identify the tone of something you've designed or an idea that remains resident in your mind?

Once you identify the tone, what is the tenor of the thing you identified?

Key differences between tone and tenor:

- **Focus:**
  - Tone: Focuses on the emotional or attitudinal aspect.
  - Tenor: Focuses on the subject matter.

- **Changeability:**
  - Tone: Can change within the same context. For example, a serious tone turning playful.
  - Tenor: Remains constant within a given context.

- **Interplay:**
  - Tone interacts with the tenor to create meaning. For example, a serious tone discussing a tragic event conveys empathy.
  - Tenor provides the context for understanding tone. Different tenors require different tones.

It is essential to note that everything designed has tone and tenor. When it becomes difficult to assign meaning to something, consider the tone and tenor you wish to project in your design.

See also:
Meaning versus Value | Music | Rhythm and Silence

While tone and tenor work in harmony, they each play a distinct role in orchestrating human expression.

Transformation
Stories have two jobs: to prompt transformation and to provoke action.

95/100

The day began with a whisped breeze, fooling anyone who knew it was tornado season. But the whisper progressed into a squall, and the bright sky darkened to a grey gloom.

A young boy stood next to his sister, holding a phone in the air as their mother explained that she'd be home as soon they reopened flooded Walnut Creek Road. She told them to brush up and tuck into bed; the storm would pass quickly.

A barn door could be heard slamming shut, interrupted by the crash of thunder that startled the boy who dropped the phone, ending the call and shattering the phone.

The children ran to their bedroom and jumped under their covers, passing a newspaper with the headline "The Clown Slayer Strikes Again". With blankets pulled up to their wide-open eyes, their mother's soon-to-be-ended storm instead grew in intensity, and then the lights went out.

With flashlights in hand, the children did what they were taught: go to the basement where they would be safe from tornados. The basement door opened with squeaks and creaks. They were headed down the steps when they heard a noise; something was alive and moving in the dark. As they got closer to the unseen sound, they embraced each other. The boy pointed his flashlight in the direction of the sound. He picked up a baseball bat that was leaning conveniently against the wall and got ready to swing.

The sound came from behind a partially closed door, and became more pronounced as the children got closer. As the boy reached for the door with the bat in hand, the family cat jumped out. And just then, the lights were restored. They laughed, embraced the cat, and relaxed. The boy dropped the bat in relief.

The children turned around and, on the steps leading to the basement, stood a clown holding an axe.

The children froze in terror. The cat had a different idea. She jumped from the boy's arms directly at the clown's face; he dropped his axe, which fell on his foot, sending him tumbling down the stairs. The children ran up the stairs to be greeted by their mother and two policemen. As the police retrieved the clown, the family cat emerged from the basement door with the clown's red nose planted on the tip of her heroic face. Despite the trauma, the reunited family laughed amid the tears.

I shared this story with a group of graduate design and film students, igniting meaningful reflections that sparked discussions about lifestyle changes. Participants voiced concerns about leaving their children home alone, crime, reconsidering home security, reasons not to live in the tornado belt, and even rethinking hiring clowns for birthday parties. This exercise demonstrated how storytelling can effectively inspire transformation.

See also:
Contrast, Beginning to End | Deceptive Cadence | The Paradox of Suspense

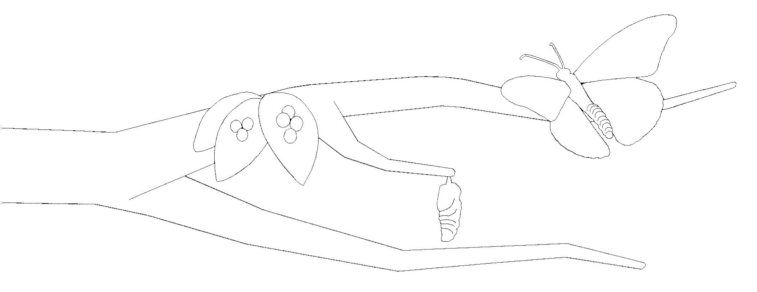

"I definitely need to update my home security system, and there's no way I'd ever leave my kids home alone. Also, I'm officially done with circuses that have clowns. And don't even get me started on the basement—I'm never going down there again!"

Verisimilitude
The appearance of being true.

96/100

Every storyteller wishes to have their story appear true or real. This holds true across genres, whether it's the far reaches of science fiction, the unlikely scenarios of romantic comedy, or design narratives that assert imminent transformations and innovations. With roots in philosophy, verisimilitude separates truth from untruths or inaccuracies.

Verisimilitude relies on the bedrock of authenticity and realism. Whether manifested through characters, settings, or dialogue, storytelling endeavors to weave a narrative that resonates as genuine and believable to its audience.

Consider, for example, a design narrative brimming with innovative concepts. While it showcases transformative ideas or promises lucrative returns, there exists a delicate equilibrium between captivating the audience and averting skepticism. It is imperative for the storyteller to maintain a narrative firmly rooted in reality, steering clear of exaggeration or sensationalism that might erode its perceived credibility. Yet, there are moments where a hint of embellishment becomes requisite to elevate a groundbreaking design into something truly extraordinary. Nonetheless, the semblance of truth must always reign supreme.

The most heroic character in a fictional story whose dialogue and characteristics mirror normalcy comes across as truthful despite the display of superhuman strength and courage. On the other hand, I recently heard a design narrative that focused on a persona that did not sound like anyone I had ever met or observed. She was too good to be true. The story and storyteller lost instant credibility; there was no perceptible verisimilitude.

There are two types of verisimilitude: cultural and generic. Cultural verisimilitude embodies the real world or life as we know it. To gain a level of cultural verisimilitude, your design narrative must reflect traditionally familiar and plausible things. Generic verisimilitude speaks to credibility through the consistency of a narrative. This simply means that, to maintain a level of truth, the story should not sway from its original premise.

To achieve verisimilitude is to:

- Offer detailed descriptions that are difficult or impossible to dispute.
- Describe any and all emotions the user of the design is expected to feel.
- Whenever something out of the ordinary or innovative is mentioned, it is a good idea to re-ground your audience with something recognizable or commonly understood.
- Always be prepared to respond to dissent with the truth.

See also:
Meaning versus Value | Narrative Intelligence | Vulnerability

Whether manifested through characters, settings,or dialogue, storytelling endeavors to weave a narrative that resonates as genuine and believable to its audience.

Vonnegut's Shapes of Stories

Kurt Vonnegut's simple yet effective story structures.

97/100

Writing a book on storytelling without a page dedicated to Kurt Vonnegut's shapes of stories would be sacrilege.

Kurt Vonnegut poses and answers the following question in his "autobiographical collage," *Palm Sunday*: "What has been my prettiest contribution to the culture?" His answer: "I would say it was a master's thesis in anthropology, which was rejected by the University of Chicago a long time ago. It was rejected because it was simple and looked like too much fun. One must not be too playful."

His underlying concept posits that stories possess identifiable structures akin to patterns on graph paper and contends that understanding the narrative structure of a society is just as "interesting as the shape of its pots and spearheads." Vonnegut's structure includes two axes. The Y axis signifies good and bad. The X axis represents the story's beginning and end. He portrays this graph with *The Man in a Hole* story. A man lives a normal life enjoying good fortune on the Y axis. The story progresses on the X axis until he falls into a hole; at this point, he is quickly met with misfortune, and the shape of his story graph drops severely. He is soon found and rescued, at which point his good fortune returns, as does the shape of his story graph.

An important note: Vonnegut conjectured that, "there's no reason these shapes couldn't be fed into computers." A man ahead of his time, he would have appreciated the University of Vermont and University of Adelaide 2016 study entitled *Six Basic Shapes Dominate the Emotional Arcs of Stories*. The study used sentiment analysis and natural language processing to consider approximately 2,000 works of fiction to determine if stories have universal shapes. It turns out that Vonnegut was correct. Not only that, but he was also able to foreshadow the coming of AI. His "Shapes of Stories" framework is simple yet ingenious, as it alleviates the intimidation factor in storytelling. I highly recommend watching the video of Vonnegut explaining his theory—it is short, to the point, and simply delightful.

Consider using this formula upon completing a design before you craft your story. Which of the eight shapes best describes your design and your design journey, as well as how the humans for whom the design is intended live their lives and how using your design will affect their lives? You might also consider using one or more of these shapes during your research stage to better plot your personas. One last thing: As you become familiar with these story shapes, it will become natural for you to recognize them in just about every story you hear or tell.

See also:
Freytag's Pyramid | The Hero's Journey | Three-Act Structure

1. Man in Hole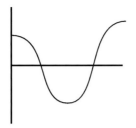

2. Boy Meets Girl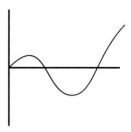

3. From Bad to Worse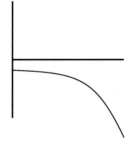

4. Which Way is Up?

5. Creation Story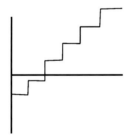

6. Old Testament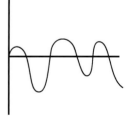

7. New Testament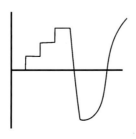

8. Cinderella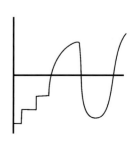

Vulnerability
Exposing one's emotions or weaknesses.

98/100

For a while, I found myself telling stories in the voice of someone I could not recognize. I was not allowing my audience to see me, and, as a result, my stories never revealed their true value, and my audience never fully understood me. When you tell your story, you are a part of it, so why not allow yourself to be seen, to be vulnerable?

Some might consider being vulnerable a weakness. In fact, it is a strength. Why? Because every human feels or is vulnerable at one time or another; when you show it, other humans will recognize this emotional exposure and connect with you. The same is true for the stories you tell about your designs and innovations.

I am encouraging writers and designers to bravely expose some level of vulnerability while telling a story.

Knowing how much to expose could be challenging. It is always helpful to break from your design narrative to speak about a challenge or encounter that posed a unique obstacle. In some situations, mentioning that you learned something new demonstrates your ability to be vulnerable. Your audience will appreciate these side moments that show you are just as susceptible to failure or being uninformed as the next guy. Let's face

it: No one is perfect, and it's always comforting to hear someone acknowledge their imperfections.

I recall a speech given by JetBlue founder David Neeleman. As he spoke about his airline's strategy, success, and errors, he also spoke about his ADHD and difficulties in reading. It was clear how the audience immediately bonded with him and, to an extent, rooted for his success.

Vulnerability does not have to be exclusively about one's personal life; it also lives in the domains of business and design. It is always powerful to speak about a fault or imperfection associated with your business or group or the design itself as long as you are able to address how the challenge is being remediated, demonstrating your ability to take these encounters head-on. It's worth repeating that humans are not infallible, and when an audience hears stories that expose vulnerabilities, they relate, connect, and trust. Another reason to open yourself up to vulnerability is that it creates a level of conflict in a story, and conflict (another storytelling principle) is an ingredient for captivating stories. All audiences enjoy being agitated by conflict and enjoy its resolution just as much.

See also:
Character Relatability | Empathy | Stimulus, Organism, Response Theory

Some might consider being vulnerable a weakness. In fact, it is a strength.

Work Backwards
Begin writing your story from the ending.

99/100

Crafting design narratives benefits from a unique advantage: we often know the ending before we begin. This familiarity allows us to employ a technique found across storytelling genres, be it fiction or nonfiction: working backward. Even when a design remains unfinished or at the proposal stage, envisioning the eventual deliverable aids in structuring the narrative from its ending. This approach proves effective as it compels us to address pivotal inquiries such as the design's purpose, its target audience, anticipated obstacles, the delineation of value (both tangible and intangible), the research influencing the final design, and the distinguishing features setting this design apart from competitive designs. Knowing your story's outcome will give you all the clues and prompts necessary for a great beginning.

Consider the following points when writing backward:

• While we typically start design projects by defining user personas and archetypes, beginning your story from the end considers additional users, stakeholders, and investors that might have been excluded.
• Starting your story from the end informs backstory, foreshadowing, and exposition, influencing the level of detail needed at the beginning. An overabundance of exposition might cause an audience to lose patience and interest. This approach better informs precisely what is necessary in exposition.
• From the end, looking forward makes it easier to identify the critical problems and opportunities faced during the design process. Some will be worth mentioning.
• Beyond the primary design goals, exploring backward may reveal secondary and tertiary objectives, broadening your design's appeal and consumer base.
• Starting from the ending often sparks greater creativity in crafting your story, possibly because it diverges from the conventional methods. It's not about telling the story in reverse, though it can be effective; it's about approaching storytelling differently, through an atypical lens.
• And finally, once you identify your ending, you will have a much better time crafting your beginning. If you capture your audience at once upon a time, you will likely keep them until you're happily ever after.

Always remember exceptional endings will always bring your audience back.

...Once Upon a Time

Happily Ever After...

World-Building
The world your humans, designs, and environments live in.

100/100

In world-building, you consider everything that exists in the world that surrounds your design. Nothing in our world exists in isolation. When examining a culture, it is essential to understand the surrounding world and the things that affect cognition, behavior, and tradition. Of course, we never want to overrun a story with too much protracted and unnecessary information; however, explaining the world your design lives in sets context, meaning, and value.

Here is a list of elements that you might consider including while building your world:

Context: Where will your design be used, sold, or discussed? If it's for a kitchen, focus on the kitchen, not just the tool.
Resources: What resources does your design need? Consider fuel, water, sunlight, etc.
Economics: Are economic factors relevant? Note if the design suits a luxury or broad-market audience, especially in tough times.
History: Does the past provide context or add meaning to your design?
Politics: Are there political or regulatory considerations?

Of course, a world could not be built without people. These are your personas, archetypes, and real humans (and other species, like pets) who will use, support, and advocate for your work. In many, if not most, cases, world-building requires diversity. There is nothing homogenous in the real world. Include elements of language, ceremonies, and rituals that bring your design to life.

World-building must also include appropriate technology that makes the world go around. This might include enabling technology, innovations, or legacy tech that will affect your design.

Education, training, and mentorship are all a natural part of world-building. Based on the complexity and familiarity of your design, consider including how consumers will become aware of your design, how to use it, and where to go for help.

Humans are always concerned with health and well-being, including physical, emotional, and mental health. Will your design contribute in one way or another to the well-being of the humans who use and advocate for your design?

The sheer expanse of our world offers designers an electrifying canvas. Picturing the environment where your design will take root is not just pivotal but downright invigorating. It's this process that infuses your design with soul, amplifying its essence and affirming its impact on the world at large.

See also:
Ceremonies and Rituals | Essence Model | Master Planning

The sheer expanse of our world offers designers an electrifying canvas. Picturing the environment where your design will take root is not just pivotal but downright invigorating. It's this process that infuses your design with soul, amplifying its essence and affirming its impact on the world at large.

Acknowledgments

Every word in this book is shaped by countless conversations, revisiting the stories and designs that have shaped my career, and the unwavering support from those who believed in me, even when I doubted myself.

To Robin, Hannah, and Benjamin: your encouragement, love, and patience with my endless musings on storytelling have been invaluable. Thank you for being there every step of the way. You are each a part of this book.

To my mentors at The American Film Institute—especially Bob Boyle and Robert Wise—thank you for transforming storytelling from a process to a passion. And to John Williams, your ability to evoke deep emotion with just two notes has been a lasting source of inspiration.

Will Lidwell and Jill Butler, your support, friendship, and optimism have been indispensable. I couldn't have done this without you—thank you.

I am deeply grateful to Jonathan Simcosky, who guided me through the intricacies of the publishing world. Your insights and support have been invaluable.

To the countless designers and storytellers I've had the privilege to lead, thank you for listening, learning, and, most importantly, teaching me something new every day.

Finally, to my parents, Edward and Dora Sandler: though they are not here to hold this book in their hands, it would not have been possible without their unwavering belief in me.

About the Designers

George Bokhua is a graphic designer with a passion for creating logos. Specializing in logo design, George believes in the power of simplicity and sophistication. His work is characterized by clean lines and thoughtful details, making each design both elegant and effective.

George's philosophy is that less is more. He focuses on stripping down designs to their essence, ensuring they communicate a clear message with a refined aesthetic. This approach has made him a sought-after designer in the world of branding.

In addition to his design work, George took on the role of layout designer for this book, *Universal Principles of Storytelling for Designers*. Alongside him as an assistant and illustrator was David Dron.

David has a background in 3D modeling from his schooling in car design. For this project, they developed an illustration style that consists of pixelated lines—a style reminiscent of work-in-progress digital sketching.

By blending his design principles with the art of storytelling, George and David have contributed to a book that is both visually engaging and informative.

About the Author

I am a storyteller and a designer—two roles that are deeply intertwined. Stories ignite design, and design inspires new stories, creating a continuous cycle that propels human progress and innovation.

The story/design connection became an "*aha*" moment during my undergraduate days at Hofstra University, where I shuffled between theatre, design, and anthropology, three disciplines that seemed to join forces effortlessly. My storytelling and design journey deepened at the American Film Institute's Center for Advanced Film Studies, where theory became practice, and I discovered a passion for designing the silent protagonist of every story— the *Mise en Scène* (principle 52). I spent time in Hollywood as an art director, crafting theatrical sets in New York, working in photographic illustration, and freelancing during the holiday season, where I designed window displays for high-end retailers.

As shared in my introduction, I found myself drawn to the lasting impact of nonfiction storytelling, particularly in the world of financial services. At Merrill Lynch, I redesigned how analysts communicated with the patrons of Wall Street, and at Goldman Sachs, I pioneered the use of UX and data visualization. I began to explore and create innovative techniques that enable humans to interact with large volumes of data efficiently, discerning hidden characteristics, patterns, and anomalies within dynamically changing information spaces (non-language, data-centric, progressive storytelling).

Later, I cofounded Brew, a design and innovation consultancy that assisted organizations to think differently, innovate, and design unique consumer experiences. I also had the honor of assisting leaders of sovereign governments in developing stories and place-based experiences that lifted their brands.

My career has spanned global leadership roles, including at NCR, where I led a diverse design portfolio encompassing industrial design, digital, ethnography, and architecture. My team and I reimagined experiences in financial services, airports, retail, and hospitality. At Aon, as Chief Design Officer, I led a talented global team, transforming brand principles into cutting-edge and profitable consumer experiences.

As a consultant, I currently help organizations reinvent themselves and grow by leveraging storytelling, design, and storythinking as catalysts for innovation.

Index